★ POPULAR MECHANICS ★

MAN*Crafts*

LEATHER TOOLING, FLY TYING, AX WHITTLING
AND OTHER COOL THINGS TO DO

HEARST BOOKS
New York

An Imprint of Sterling Publishing
387 Park Avenue South
New York, NY 10016

ISBN 978-1-61837-164-5

Distributed in Canada by Sterling Publishing
c/o Canadian Manda Group, 165 Dufferin Street
Toronto, Ontario, Canada M6K 3H6

Distributed in the United Kingdom by GMC Distribution Services
Castle Place, 166 High Street, Lewes, East Sussex, England BN7 1XU

Distributed in Australia by Capricorn Link (Australia) Pty. Ltd.
P.O. Box 704, Windsor, NSW 2756, Australia

For information about custom editions, special sales, and premium and corporate purchases, please contact Sterling Special Sales at 800-805-5489 or specialsales@sterlingpublishing.com.

Manufactured in China

2 4 6 8 10 9 7 5 3 1

www.sterlingpublishing.com

★ POPULAR MECHANICS ★

MAN*Crafts*

❖

LEATHER TOOLING, FLY TYING, AX WHITTLING AND OTHER COOL THINGS TO DO

HEARST BOOKS
New York

�֍ CONTENTS ✦

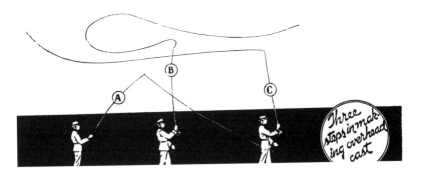

Three steps in making overhead cast

✦ INTRODUCTION ✦

The end of World War II brought equal measures of heart-felt relief and enthusiastic hope for a prosperous future. The brave returning servicemen—along with the civilians who had served so selflessly on the home front—understood that they had won a war not just with weapons, but with resourcefulness, skills, and plain old hard work. These men brought the can-do attitude that had helped them save the world back to their new jobs, setting aside wartime weapons and skills to master brand-new abilities, equipment, and materials in trades such as leatherworking, sign lettering, and bookbinding. They already had what they needed—what any man needs—for success. Their experiences had taught them that when it came to making a future for themselves and their families, the best tools were right at hand.

Popular Mechanics was there to help. Back in the early days of the postwar period, we produced a series of step-by-step booklets to help the independent-minded man hone his craft skills and use those skills to develop a successful small business.

We've revived and updated the information in those publications and present the best projects here. The instructions are intended not only to help the industrious man create a hand-worked item of value, but also learn essential skills along the way. The illustrations and text re-created here will seem wonderfully nostalgic, but they're as practical and useful now as they were when we first published them.

And though most men today won't be turning to crafts for a living, they can certainly take every bit as much pride in these interesting and rewarding crafts as hobbies. Today's often uninspired mass-produced goods leave plenty of room for the exceptional quality and originality of handcrafted goods.

Some of these crafts, such as sign lettering, may not seem applicable in today's world, but the beauty of these skills is that they are transferable. Learn how to letter a sign, and you develop enviable penmanship that will be closer to art than to craft. You can even use those skills in home projects, such as a stenciled border of words around a bedroom.

The projects themselves are both challenging and fun, and the diversity offers something for every man. The woodworker will leap at the chance to learn about the practical items that can come to life under the blade of a coping saw. Are you an avid outdoorsman? If so, the chapter on tying flies will pique your interest. For unusual projects, look no further than axe-crafting or tin-can creations. Of course there's plenty for the traditionalist in these pages, whether you want to explore classic leatherworking, rebind a book, or knot a lanyard.

Even if you don't want to leap right in with both hands and start sawing a pair of bookends or tooling a new leather wallet, you're sure to enjoy the distinctive style of writing that evokes the tenor of those simpler, optimistic times. Just reading this book will take you back to the very start of the Baby Boom, when men made what they needed and made money making what others needed. So make a little time for an incredibly enjoyable trip to the past, courtesy of the *Popular Mechanic* archives.

The Editors of *Popular Mechanics*

COPING SAW CARPENTRY

Here is a craft that has proven increasingly popular throughout the United States during the last few years. Aside from being a fascinating hobby, it can be made to produce a steady income for the worker at home. Requiring fewer tools than any other known craft and only the cheapest of scrap materials, it demands a minimum of space, time, and labor and is easily mastered within a short time by the novice. Its products enjoy a steady market and are limited only by the imagination of the worker.

Hundreds of different articles of both utilitarian and decorative value can be created through knowledge of this craft. A careful study of this section and close application in following each step of the work described here will produce a basic knowledge sufficient to start the worker into remunerative fields.

Carpentry has a great number of specialties, such as construction, inlay, cabinets, etc., but of them all Coping Saw Carpentry is the easiest in which to get started. It requires nothing more than a coping saw, sandpaper, paints, paper, pencil, and scrap wood. Joints, as in all carpentry, are either nailed, screwed, or glued together, although many finished articles of this specialty require but one piece of material.

This section has been divided into four sections for clarity. The first deals with a description of required tools and materials. This is followed by step-by-step instructions for the completion of two articles. The third section covers instructions for the use of a graph. This is a method by which any drawing or illustration can be reproduced on the wood in any desired size. The last section consists of illustrated suggestions for other articles.

Few Americans have traveled along our highways without seeing the large displays of lawn figures, weather vanes, door stops, plant sticks, garden markers, book ends, etc., which tempt the motorist. These are the "shops" of the coping saw carpenters who have created a new, fascinating and highly remunerative industry in America. It has become the sole vocation to a great many, while countless others, having fun at home in their spare time, add appreciably to their regular incomes. Why not join them and master this new craft while still in its infancy? Let's go!

✤ TOOLS AND MATERIALS ✤

The Coping Saw. A coping saw consists of a steel frame in the form of a large, wide "U" with a fine saw blade fastened between its ends, as shown in Fig. 1. It is designed expressly for cutting curves, circles, and inside areas in thin wood.

The blade is attached by inserting its ends in the slots of the saw frame. Attach one end of the blade in the slot at the handle end of the frame. Place the other end of the frame against the body, squeeze the ends inward by pressure on the handle, insert the other end of the blade in the slot against the body, and release the pressure. The spring in the saw frame will tighten the blade.

While such a saw can be worked in practically any position, it is usually used as shown in Fig. 2. The required pressure on the handle will vary with the thickness of the wood being cut. When being used in a vertical position, as shown in Fig. 2, the pressure is naturally light, and if the wood is extremely thin the weight of the saw is often sufficient. In such a case the weight of the saw will carry it on its downward stroke and the holding hand merely acts as a guide. Care must be taken not to "overload" the blade and break it. Such breakage necessitates a quantity of extra blades being kept in stock.

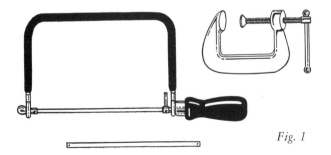

Fig. 1

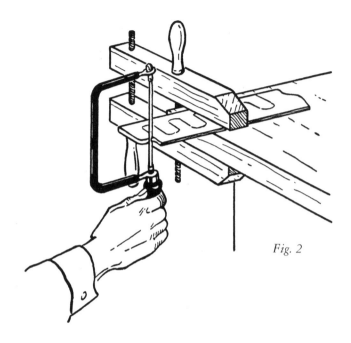

Fig. 2

The sawing of "inside" areas is a simple process. Carefully punch or bore a small hole through the area to be removed. Unfasten the outer end of the blade, insert it through the hole, refasten the blade, and the saw is ready for the work. Study Fig. 2 and then practice curves, circles, and inside cuts on various thicknesses of scrap wood until you become completely familiar with the saw and its use.

Clamps. As it is necessary to hold the work firmly over the edge of the bench or table when sawing, a clamp is required. See Fig. 2. The wood clamp shown in this illustration is recommended, as its wide jaws will not injure the surface of the wood. The small clamp shown in Fig. 1 may be used, but pieces of scrap material must be inserted between the steel jaws and the wood being held to prevent the jaws from marring the surface.

Pencil and Paper. The only use for pencil and paper in this work is the copying and transferring of designs to the wood. Any light grade paper can be used and a No. 2 pencil is recommended. The method of copying designs will be found on Page 19 under "Obtaining Designs." The transfer of a design to the wood is a simple process. When the copy has been completed, turn the paper over and shade it heavily with pencil marks on the back. This acts as a carbon. See Fig. 3. The paper is then turned over with the shading next to the wood, and the original lines of the design retraced with the pencil, which in turn transfers them to the wood by means of the shading, as shown in Fig. 4.

Sandpaper. Three grades of sandpaper will serve for this work. These are No. 0 (fine), No. ½ (medium), and No. 1½ (medium coarse). Always scrub with the grain of the wood and never across or against it. Use the coarse paper first and then finish with the fine. Wrap the paper around a small wood block when sanding flat surfaces.

Wood. Thin wood ranging from ⅟₁₆-inch to 1-inch in thickness is used for this work Small crates, packing boxes, thin plywood,

Fig. 3

Fig. 4

veneers, cigar boxes, and similar box lumber are ideal. As most coping saw articles are small, scraps of all sizes and shapes may be utilized. Larger articles are naturally made of thicker stock.

Glue and Nails. Any good liquid glue will suffice for this work, and as most articles are made of thin stock, ¼-inch to 1-inch brads should be used.

Paints and Brushes. While lacquer or enamel is recommended, any good oil paint will serve. The former, best hides such defects as cracks, joints, sandpaper marks, and other surface blemishes. Small cans of red, blue, yellow, black, and white are sufficient. Two camel's-hair brushes are desirable. One should be small and pointed such as a No. 3 for fine line work, while a No. 10 wash brush is best for large areas.

✤ BOOK ENDS ✤

Step 1. Rule a 5-inch by 8-inch sheet of paper with 1-inch squares, as shown in Fig. 6. This is called a "graph." The lines of the original are now copied square by square on this paper. When doing this, see that the line you are drawing on your paper passes through each square in exactly the same location as the corresponding line passes through the same squares of Fig. 6. Complete both figures in this manner.

Step 2. Turn the paper over and shade its back with heavy pencil marks, as shown in Fig. 3 and explained under "Pencil and Paper" on page 13.

Step 3. Two ⅛-inch thick, 3-inch wide, and 5-inch long pieces of wood are required for the figures. Should ⅛-inch stock be

unobtainable, any stock up to ½-inch can be substituted. The two bases of the book ends are each ¾-inch thick, 4-inch wide, and 5-inch long, while the two uprights measure ¾-inch thick, 4-inch wide, and 4-inch long.

Step 4. Each of the base and upright pieces must be cut to exact size, and all edges and both surfaces carefully sanded. The upright is glued to the base and reinforced with brads driven through the base into the edge of the upright. Complete both assemblies, remove excess glue, and finish by sanding.

Step 5. Carefully sand each face of the two figure pieces, leaving their edges untouched.

Step 6. The design of each figure is now transferred to the wood. Place the paper with its shaded side down on the wood, and trace over the lines with a sharp pencil. Remove the paper when finished and retrace over the lines with the pencil on the bare wood. Make the tracing on both sides of each piece, as in Fig. 4, reversing the pattern for the back of the figure.

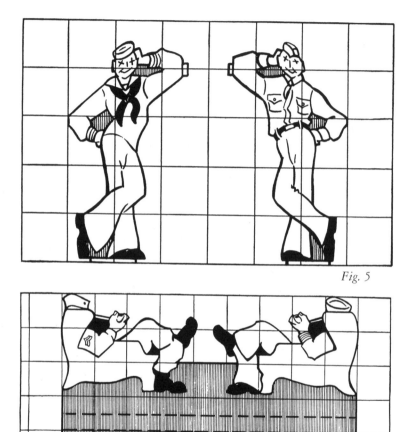

Fig. 5

Fig. 6

Step 7. Both pieces are now cut out with the coping saw. Assemble the piece for sawing, as shown in Fig. 2. Saw just outside the lines. Be sure to leave the small lugs at the feet and elbow, as shown in Fig. 5.

Step 8. Sand all edges of both cut-outs smooth to their lines.

Step 9. Give the book ends two coats of green paint. Paint the soldier's clothes khaki by mixing white with a touch of red and blue and quite a bit of yellow. The same mixture with less white will produce a brown for the shoes. The areas shown by shading should be green. All outlines are in black. Paint both sides in the same manner. The sailor's clothes are white with a black tie, black outlines, and black shoes. Shaded areas are green. Paint both sides in the same manner.

Step 10. Place each figure on its book end and mark the location of its lugs on the base and upright. Cut out small holes for these, apply glue, and slip the figures in place. Remove excess glue and allow to dry.

Step 11. If felt or any green cloth, such as black-out material, is available, cut 4-inch by 5-inch pieces and glue them to the under side of each base piece.

✥ PIPE RACK ✥

Step 1. Rule a 7-inch by 9-inch piece of paper with 1-inch squares, as shown in Fig. 6. Complete a copy of both pieces shown in the manner explained in Step 1 for the Book Ends.

Step 2. Follow instructions given for Step 2 for the Book Ends.

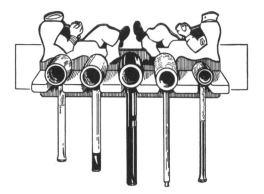

Step 3. Two blocks of wood are required for this pipe rack. The back is ¼-inch thick, 4 ½-inch wide, and 9-inch long. The rack is ½-inch thick, 2-inch wide, and 9-inch long.

Step 4. Follow instructions given in Step 5 for the Book Ends.

Step 5. The design of each piece is now transferred to its wood, as explained in Step 6 for the Book Ends.

Step 6. Both pieces are now cut out with the coping saw. Assemble each piece for sawing, as shown in Fig. 2. Saw just outside the lines.

Step 7. Follow Step 8 of the Book Ends.

Step 8. Paint the soldier and sailor as given in Step 9 for the Book Ends. Paint the chairs red and the balance of the back in green. Paint the rack green. Assemble the rack to the back along the dotted lines shown in Fig. 6. Do this with glue and brads driven through the back into the edge of the rack. Both faces of the rack should be painted, but only the front face of the back.

Step 9. Carefully drive two small nails through the neutral areas between the pipes and the arms for hanging.

✤ OBTAINING DESIGNS ✤

Designs suitable for coping saw work may be obtained from a number of sources. Story and advertisement illustrations from newspapers, magazines, picture books, and travel folders provide good ones. While many of these will be found either too large or too small for the particular article you may wish to make, a simple method may be used to reproduce them the exact size you wish to have them.

As an example, let us say that the design you have chosen measures 6-inch wide and 6-inch long, but you wish your article to be only 3-inch square. Over the original design draw 1-inch squares. This is called a "graph," and is used to aid in making freehand copies of any design. On a sheet of blank paper rule ½-inch squares. This is done because you wish your copy to be just half the size of the original from which you are copying.

The lines of the original are then copied square by square on the blank paper you have just ruled. When doing this, see that the line you are drawing on your paper passes through each square in exactly the same location as the corresponding line passes through the same squares on the original design. In this manner a copy of any design may be drawn freehand to any desired size. If you wish your copy to be twice the size of the original, the paper should be ruled with squares twice as large as those ruled on the original. If it is to be once and a half as large, the squares should be once and a half as large, etc.

By this simple method, any picture, drawing, design, or other illustration can be utilized for tracing purposes.

✧ SUGGESTED ARTICLES ✧

Here are a few suggestions for articles easily created with the coping saw:

Door stops
Utensil racks
Glass coasters
Napkin rings
Number plates
Tie racks
Pencil trays
Letter racks
Book ends
Pipe racks
Tooth brush holders
Place card holders
Garden markers
Letter knives
Jig saw puzzles
Bread boards
Wastepaper baskets
Lampshades
Lawn figures
Memo pad holders

❖ PHOTO-BROOCH ❖

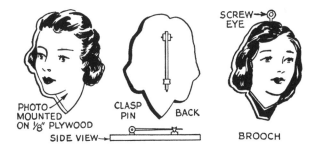

PHOTO MOUNTED ON ⅛" PLYWOOD

CLASP PIN   BACK

SIDE VIEW →

SCREW → EYE

BROOCH

❖ SHIP PLAQUE ❖

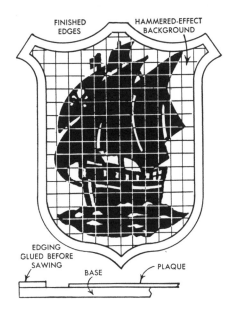

FINISHED EDGES

HAMMERED-EFFECT BACKGROUND

EDGING GLUED BEFORE SAWING

BASE

PLAQUE

❖ PICTURE FRAMES ❖

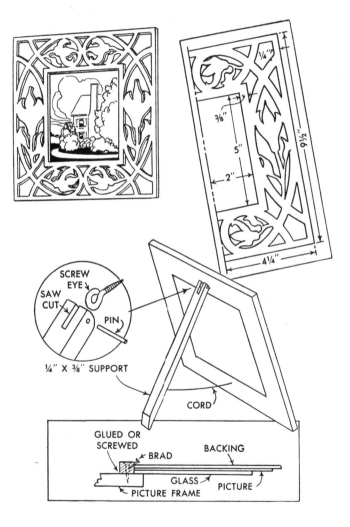

1/4"''

9½"

3/8"''

5"''

2"''

4¼"''

SCREW EYE

SAW CUT

PIN

¼" X ⅜" SUPPORT

CORD

GLUED OR SCREWED

BRAD

BACKING

GLASS

PICTURE

PICTURE FRAME

✧ MISCELLANEOUS ITEMS ✧

WASTE BASKET

PEN TRAY

LETTER RACK

SIGNS

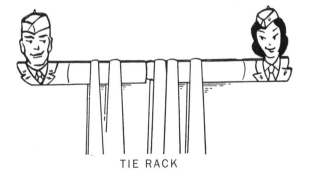

TIE RACK

LEATHERCRAFT

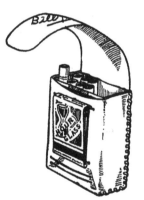

Centuries before the art of weaving cloth was known, our ancestors were using leather in many ways. Footwear, clothing, shelter and even drinking vessels were provided by the sun-cured, shaggy hides of animals that had been felled with clubs or stone arrows or that had been trapped. Early explorers of America found the native people quite skillful in the art of tanning leather, but no one can say when or how they gained their knowledge and skill. They were found to be especially adept in making buckskin, which has never been equaled for its softness and water shedding ability.

Among our earliest American colonists we find a great many leather craftsmen, and from them has sprung one of our great industries of today. The curing, working, and beautifying of leather has proved of such value in modern life that many of our necessities such as shoes, coats, gloves and hats are made of it. Demand has created a ready market for leather luxury items as well, and we find belts, pocketbooks, luggage, book bindings, portfolios, bags, desk sets, picture frames, and similar items flooding the counters of our finest stores.

The working of leather is not a difficult craft to master, but as with anything else it requires certain knowledge of basic principles and accepted practices. It is not an expensive craft, requires few tools, and its materials are easily obtainable. As an aid to the beginner, this section has been divided into a discussion of basic tools and materials followed by step-by-step instructions for completing one article in leather. If these are followed closely and the worker masters each step as he actually makes the article, he will experience no difficulty in carrying on the work into new and greater fields. While the article given here was chosen for instructional purposes primarily because it required a majority of the basic operations in leathercraft, it was also designed to give the beginner an item of real utilitarian value for his first attempts. Make sure that each step of the work is thoroughly understood before proceeding with the next. As a further aid in helping the beginner to carry on alone after completion of this first article, a splendid book on the subject will be found in your public library.

✤ TOOLS ✤

Revolving Punch. This tool is used for punching the holes in leather required for eyelets, belts and lacings. It is equipped with six tube punches of varying sizes. Such a tool is of great convenience, but not a necessity as the drive punch, shown in Fig. 1 at "C," can be substituted for it. The revolving punch should be tested until mastered on scrap leather. Always mark with pencil or awl the exact location of the hole, and then center the tube over the mark and punch the hole. It may be necessary to move the punch back and forth while still closed on the leather to complete the cut. Such a punch is shown in Fig. 1 at "A."

Skiving Knife. Skiving is the thinning of leather at edges where it is to be sewed or laced, or the thinning of portions or areas at which it is to be folded. Edges to be joined with lacing or sewing are skived so that when both are placed together they will be no thicker than the thickness of a single piece. The most popular type of skiving knife is shown in Fig. 1 at "B." Such a knife is also used for all general cutting purposes. It should be kept razor sharp at all times. Skiving is done on the flesh side of the leather.

Place the edge of the leather on the edge of a glass, marble or hard wood base. Slice off thin pieces of about 2-inch in length and ¾-inch in width. Keep testing the thickness as the work progresses. Practice on scraps until full confidence is gained. Whenever cutting leather guide the knife along a straight edge, such as a steel square or ruler, for straight cuts. Curves and circles must be cut free-hand.

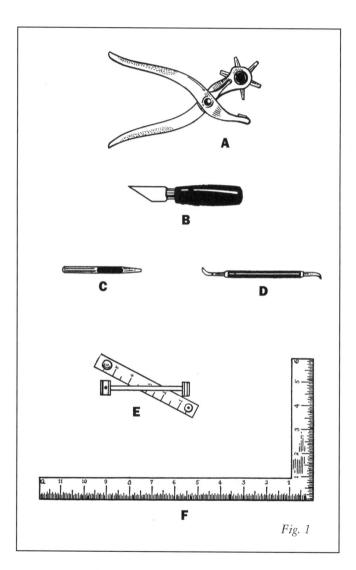

A

B

C

D

E

F

Fig. 1

Drive Punch. A drive punch, such as shown in Fig. 1 at "C," is used for punching holes which cannot be reached with the revolving punch, or when a revolving punch is not available. It can be had in several sizes. To use such a punch, place it on the marked hole location and strike it with a hammer or mallet, as shown in Fig. 5.

Modeler. While a "tracer" tool can be purchased, one will not be necessary for this work, as the small end of the modeler can be used for tracing designs on leather. The "spade" end, which is broad, is used for embossing and putting down design backgrounds. Handle the modeler as you would a pencil. Only time and practice will teach the worker proper pressure control on the tool while doing outline tooling, flat modeling, or embossing. Such a tool is shown in Fig. 1 "D."

Snap Attaching Set. Snap buttons are found on small articles, such as key cases and coin purses, while larger projects, such as large ladies' bags, are usually equipped with bag plates. To properly set snaps in leather you will need one of these attaching sets, such as shown in Fig. 1 at "E." The ruled piece is known as the "anvil," while the other piece is the "hammer."

Steel Square. This is an important item among the tools required for leathercraft. It is used for lay-outs and leather cutting, squaring-up and measuring.

Cutting Board. A hard wood, maple board is recommended for leather work. This is used for almost all operations, such as lay-out, design transfer, cutting, tooling, etc.

✤ MATERIALS ✤

Aside from the actual leather used in the project and possible lacing, the required list of materials will depend on the type of article being made. Such items as key plates, various types and widths of lacing, snap buttons, eyelets, buckles, linings, etc., will be indicated by the article itself and should be obtained before the article is started.

✤ CIGARETTE AND MATCH CASE ✤

The cigarette case shown on page 25 has two innovations of interest to the owner. Unlike the usual run of such cases, this one provides a holder for book matches and has the signature of the owner tooled across its flap. A close study of the finished case will prove of great value to the beginner. It is made of one piece of leather, requires a minimum of lacing, and can be completed in approximately an hour. Each step is fully explained below, so get busy and "make your own."

Step 1. A pattern for the case is shown in Fig. 3. This is drawn on squares representing 1-inch each. To copy full size, rule a

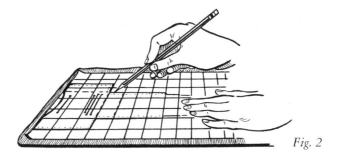

Fig. 2

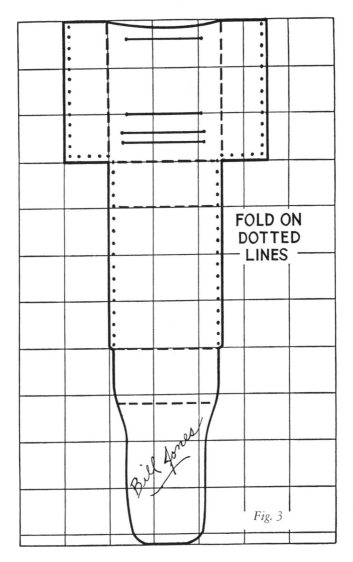

FOLD ON
DOTTED
LINES

Bill Jones

Fig. 3

sheet of paper with 1-inch squares of the same number as those shown in Fig. 3. Such a plan is called a "graph." Its squares aid the worker in copying it. When doing this, see that the line you are drawing on your paper passes through each square in exactly the same location as the corresponding line passes through the same squares of Fig. 3. Use your ruler or steel square to make all straight lines. Broken lines indicate bends and need not be copied. The dots shown around the edges are punch or slit hole locations for the lacing, and should be copied. The four slits shown near the top must be laid out with great care, as these form the match and flap holders. Keeping in mind that the lower portion of the pattern forms the flap of the finished case, write your signature across it high enough to permit the end of the flap to go into its holder without covering the signature.

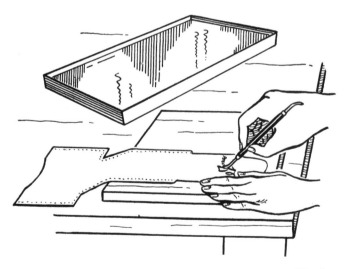

Fig. 4

Step 2. Obtain a piece of leather approximately 5-inch wide and 1½-inch long. The pattern is now transferred to the leather. There are two methods of doing this work. A simple way is to shade the back of your pattern with pencil marks along the lines showing through. This is then placed on the leather and the original lines retraced with a pencil, as shown in Fig. 2. The better practice, however, is to dampen the leather on its flesh, or unfinished side, by patting it with a sponge dipped in cold water. Continue until the finished side turns dark indicating enough moisture. Always dampen the entire surface of the leather, even though only a small part of it is to be tooled, as this insures against possible color changes, water marks and uneven shrinkage once the leather dries. Some workers prefer the dip method of wetting their leather. This is done with the aid of a shallow pan, as shown in Fig. 4. Holding one corner with the finger tips, quickly pass it through the bath three or four times, with its finished side down. Do not allow the leather to soak in the bath. It is then carefully shaken out and placed flat on a piece of glass, marble or hard wood. Care must be taken to see that the finished side of the leather is up, as this is the side on which tooling and outline work is done. Center the pattern with the design side up on the leather, as shown in Fig. 2. The lines of the pattern are now transferred to the leather with the modeling tool. The small end of the modeler is used for this purpose, and should be held in the hand exactly as a pencil, as shown in Fig. 4. Go over each line with a firm even stroke. Lift the corner of your pattern from time to time to see that all lines are being impressed clearly on the leather. As with the first method, use your steel square to trace straight lines and insure squared corners when required. All curves must be made freehand. Carefully remove the pattern but do not move the leather from its base.

Step 3. While the leather is damp and in position on a firm base, the signature is tolled on it, as shown in Fig. 4. Doing this at this time eliminates redampening the piece later. Do this work with the small end of the modeler directly on the finished side of the leather. See that your lines are clear but not too deep. When the signature has been tooled, allow the piece to dry on its base without moving it. Leather takes the shape it is in when wet once it has dried, so it is important that it be allowed to dry in a flat position. As a final check, inspect all lines to see that they are clear. Go over any too faint to easily follow. It must be remembered that the outline of the pattern need be only clear enough to permit cutting, while those of the signature remain as a decoration.

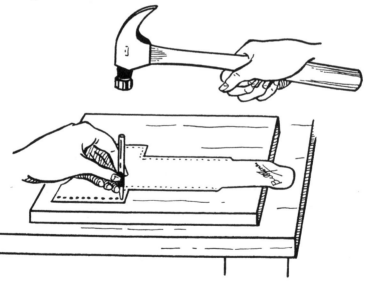

Fig. 5

Step 4. When the leather has become thoroughly dried, the pattern is cut out. This is done with the skiving knife and steel square. Place the leather on a flat wood surface. Maple is recommended for a cutting board, as its fine straight grain will not deflect the cutting blade. All cuts should be made directly over the pencil or tool lines. Use the knife at approximately the same angle as a pencil is held when writing. Hold the square firmly on the line when cutting, and make each cut go entirely through the leather on the first stroke. Curves must be made free-hand with great care. A sharp pair of tin snips can be used, if handy, for cutting curvatures in leather. Cut around the entire outside of the pattern, and then follow this by cutting the four slits appearing near the top of the pattern. Note that the two slits forming the flap holder are slightly longer than those holding the book of matches.

Step 5. The holes are now punched for lacing. See that these are in a straight line and if not lay the steel square along them and re-mark each. If the revolving punch is being used, start with the top and work down each side. The drive punch is shown being used in Fig. 5. If this is used, place the leather on the hard wood block. Complete all holes at this time. The size of the hole will depend on the size of the lacing being used.

Step 6. The edges of the piece that have just been punched are now skived. As two thicknesses of leather are to be joined along these edges, each edge must be skived to half the thickness of the original leather. This is necessary so that when the pieces are brought together they will match in thickness the rest of the holder. Do this work on the flesh side of the leather, and make sure that the skiving knife is extremely sharp. The process has been explained before under "Skiving Knife." Follow the

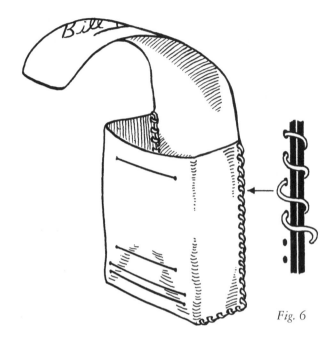

Fig. 6

instructions carefully. If a very heavy leather is being used, it should be slightly skived on the flesh side along the portions being bent, as shown in Fig. 3 by broken lines. These should be along each dotted, or broken line, and about 1-inch in width. Cuts should be about one-fourth the thickness of the leather.

After this skiving has been done along all broken lines, test each one to see that it folds easily. Do not crease the fold at this time.

Step 7. Leather is dyed for several different reasons. Where cut edges show up against the color of the leather being used, dye should be applied to conceal them. If a natural leather is being used, this will not be necessary, but it is often desirable to dye a natural leather some other color. A third use of dyes is to bring out designs in color. Thus, if the worker wishes to have his signature appear in color, he should dye the letters, or if his cut edges show "raw" against the finished side of his case, these should be touched up with dye to make them match the finished side. There are two types of dyes on the market. Water dye is the most popular. It comes in powdered form and is mixed with hot water. The piece may be dipped in this solution, or the dye applied with a camel hair brush. Oil stains produce good color on leather in softened effects. It is first thinned with turpentine, applied to the leather, and then immediately wiped off. Before any dyeing can be done, the leather must be thoroughly cleaned with a good cleaning solution. When the leather is almost dry the dye is applied. Test for color on scrap leather before applying the dye on your finished piece. If too light after drying, apply a second coat. Complete by polishing with a soft cloth.

Step 8. The case is now ready for lacing. Cut a block of wood the size of a cigarette package. Fold the case along each broken line, as shown in Fig. 3. If these have been carefully skived, no trouble should be had in creasing each fold. Place the block in the case and go over all edges for right angle folds. Some prefer to wrap a mallet or hammer with cloth and tap these folds until they are well creased. There are a number of different types of lacing, but the one used on this case is by far the most common. It is known as the "whip" stitch. When using this type, cut your lacing three times as long as the distance being laced. Two lengths of approximately 12 inches will be required, as both sides measure 4 inches each.

To properly hide and hold the start and finish of a lacing, its ends may be either cemented between the pieces being laced or threaded under several stitches. To do this neatly, the ends must be skived to prevent bulging. Skive one end of the lacing leather ½-inch back. Either cement it along the inside edge of the bottom portion of the case, or lay it in such a position that the first three stitches will be threaded over it and hold it in position. Start at the bottom of the case and lace along it and then up the side, as shown in Fig. 6. Note the whip stitch, as shown in Fig. 6 at the right. When the end is in position, bring the lace through one hole, over the edge, and then through the corresponding hole in the second piece being joined. Continue this along the bottom of the case. When the corner is reached, it will be necessary to go through the corner holes twice with the lacing, so that a stitch will be on the bottom and a second one will start the side stitching from these corner holes. Continue up the side. Pull the lacing through each hole until tight against the leather of the case. Finish the stitching by skiving the last ½-inch of the lace, which is cut to proper length when the last hole is reached, and either cement or thread it to the inside of the case. Complete both sides in this manner.

Step 9. Replace the wood block in the case and tap all laced edges lightly with a smooth faced hammer. This will flatten the lacing, make it uniform, and crease the corners. Close the flap and tap the creases it makes to insure good neat folding. Complete the case by giving it a washing with saddle soap. Apply the soap in small amounts with a damp cloth. Allow it to dry for a few minutes and then polish the leather with a soft cloth. This completes the cigarette case.

✤ BILL FOLD ✤

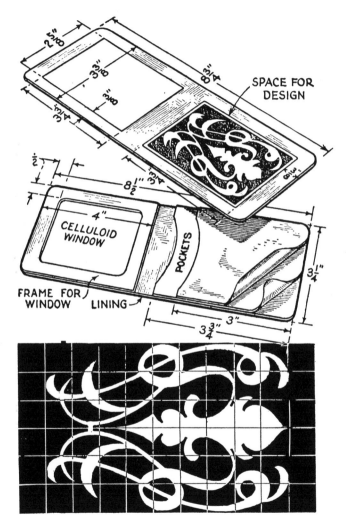

SPACE FOR DESIGN

CELLULOID WINDOW

POCKETS

FRAME FOR WINDOW

LINING

✦ MOCCASINS ✦

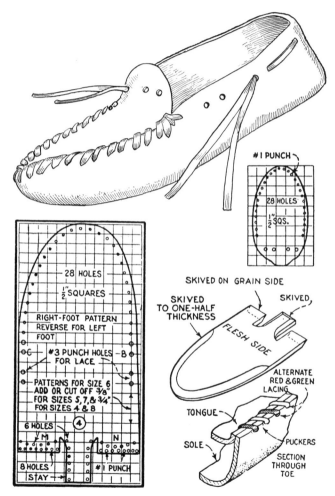

#1 PUNCH

28 HOLES

½" SQS.

28 HOLES

½" SQUARES

RIGHT-FOOT PATTERN
REVERSE FOR LEFT
FOOT

#3 PUNCH HOLES
FOR LACE

PATTERNS FOR SIZE 6
ADD OR CUT OFF ⅜"
FOR SIZES 5, 7, & ¾"
FOR SIZES 4 & 8

6 HOLES

④

M   N   N

8 HOLES   #1 PUNCH

STAY

SKIVED ON GRAIN SIDE

SKIVED
TO ONE-HALF
THICKNESS

SKIVED

FLESH SIDE

ALTERNATE
RED & GREEN
LACING

TONGUE

PUCKERS

SOLE

SECTION
THROUGH
TOE

✤ BELTS ✤

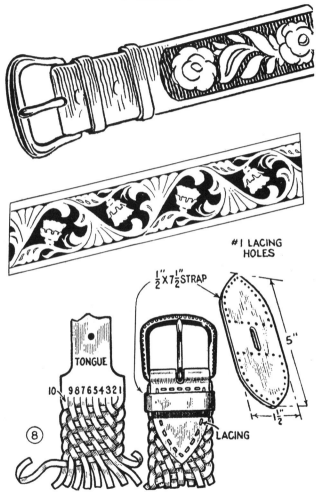

#1 LACING HOLES

½" X 7½" STRAP

5"

1½"

TONGUE

10 9 8 7 6 5 4 3 2 1

⑧

LACING

BOOKBINDING

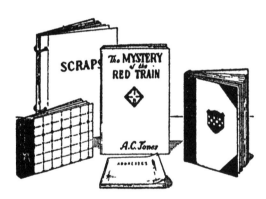

Book binding is an art of long standing as well as one of the most interesting, useful and lucrative of all the crafts. It has an added value under present conditions. The natural economies of today have greatly curtailed the manufacture of the ordinary large, cloth-bound book for commercial purposes.

Paper shortages throughout the world have made it necessary to return to the old "dime novel" of yesterday, which consisted of a small paper-bound book of light stock. These have been found ideal for use, as they may be manufactured, handled, packed and shipped with a minimum of cost, labor, space and weight. They are to the publisher what the V-mail is to the post office. Their pliable covers and small size are great advantages when packing away in barracks bags or carrying in uniform pockets, but quickly become disadvantages when attempting to keep them in a permanent and good condition.

Thousands of these little books find appreciative owners who wish to keep them permanently, and the answer to this problem is to rebind them with stiff, cloth covers, which will keep them protected from the unpredictable living conditions of the soldier. Book binding not only includes the making of permanent covers for bound books, but also stiff covers for loose-leaf binders. Magazines, clippings, snap shots, records and other data can be safely kept in such binders, so it is important for the craftsman to also master this phase of the craft. Both types of binding are covered in this booklet.

No tools will be required for this craft, except such common items as a pencil, ruler and scissors. The materials required consist of binding cardboard, covering cloth, leather or decorative paper, lining paper, buckram and paste. While all these items are manufactured for book binding work, all of them can be substituted by ordinary articles easily found.

✤ MATERIALS ✤

Covering Material. The cardboard forming the stiff covers of books is usually covered with cloth, leather or decorative paper. Natural linen, muslin or any other cloth of medium weight can be used for this purpose. Morocco, ostrich, sheepskin, suedes and steer hide are the best covering leathers for book binding. Many interesting and decorative effects can be obtained by using some of the modern decorative papers on the market today. These may be of either medium or heavy weight. Whatever material is used, all lettering, block printing or painting which will appear on the cover must be applied before the covering is mounted on the cardboard binding. It is then pasted in place.

Binding Cardboard. While it may be quite impossible to purchase regular binder board in your present location, a short discussion of this material will aid in acquainting the worker with future possibilities. Any medium or heavy cardboard can be substituted for this work, but the reader should know what is usually available in the markets in large cities. Cardboard for book binding can be found on packages, inside crating, paper boxes, etc. The manufactured article is usually carried by art and stationery stores. There are two types of book binding cardboard. One is known as "News Board" or "Chip Board," while the second is called "Binder's Board." The latter is recommended, if obtainable, for this work, as it is stiffer and superior to "News Board." It comes in large 26-inch by 36-inch sheets and its thickness comes in six standard sizes.

These are as follows:

.212" (appx. $\frac{1}{5}$")	.085" (appx. $\frac{1}{12}$")
.142" (appx. $\frac{1}{7}$")	.070" (appx. $\frac{1}{14}$")
.106" (appx. $\frac{1}{10}$")	.060" (appx. $\frac{1}{16}$")

The thickness of the cardboard of a binding depends on the size of the binder or book. A small binding, such as the "pocket" edition we are discussing in this book, will not require the thickness that must be given the binding of a large book.

Lining Paper. Two lining papers are required for each book. Each is a double page with one half covering the inside of the cardboard binding and the opposite half forming a page by itself. The former is called either the "inside front page" or the "inside back page." The latter is known as a "fly-leaf." Each paper is called the "end paper" of a book. These are usually of the same color as the cover, and slightly heavier than the pages of the printed text. While regular lining papers are supplied by art and stationery stores, practically any paper of good weight can be substituted for the manufactured article. Each lining paper must be the length of tone of the pages in the book being covered and twice as wide.

Hinge Cloth. The hinge of a book cover is made of a thin material pasted to the back of the book's pages and to the inside of the front and back covers. Buckram is usually used for this purpose. It is a coarse linen, but any strong, light cloth may be used, such as cheese cloth, cotton from a handkerchief, etc.

Paste. Bookbinder's paste can be purchased on the market, but an ordinary office variety may be substituted. This is used for mounting the covering material, lining papers and hinge cloth.

This completes the list of necessary items for binding a book. For instructional purposes, one of the small "pocket" editions has been chosen, as these are by far the most plentiful around any camp, post or station. Follow each step as given here and no difficulty will be experienced.

✤ BINDING A BOOK ✤

Step 1. The first step in preparing a book for its new cover is to remove the old one carefully. As the old cover is of paper, a safety razor blade should be used. Care must be taken, however, not to cut away any of the threads that stitch the pages together. When removing the cover, the various advertising pages so often appearing in such books can also be removed. Start with the front cover and take off the cover, the lining page and the first advertising page. Bend them back with great care and run the edge of your razor blade along their inside edges, cutting all of them away at the same time. Proceed in the same manner with the back cover, lining page and any others you wish to remove in preparation for your binding. When the covers have been removed, the inside reading matter is known as the "filler" of the book, while the covers are called the "binder."

Step 2. Before any work is done other than removing the old cover, careful dimensions must be taken of the book without its cover. Measure the length and width of the filler, and then measure its saddle, or across the back to obtain its thickness. The binding of a book should protrude beyond its leaves ⅛-inch on all sides except the back. It will therefore be necessary to add ¼-inch to its length measurement and ⅛-inch to its width. Its thickness remains as measured, although ½-inch must be added to the length of the cloth when cutting it, as shown in Fig. 3. For instructional purposes, the book chosen and illustrated here measured 6½-inch long, 4⅛-inch wide and ¾-inch thick. These dimensions must be changed to fit the particular book you are binding, but will be carried through in this text for illustrative purposes. By adding the required overlap of the binding, each cover must be cut

4 ¼-inch wide and 6 ¾-inch long. When these measurements have been taken, jot them down for future reference.

Step 3. The binding material is now chosen. This may be leather, cloth or decorative paper. In any case, a single piece must be cut to permit fitting in the filler. The length must be the length of the filler plus 2-inch for turn-over flaps and ¼-inch for a ⅛-inch extension at top and bottom. The width must be twice the width of the filler plus the filler's thickness plus ¼-inch for extensions plus ½-inch for back play and finally an added 2 inches for over-turned flaps. Follow these dimensions in Fig. 3. Cut a sheet of plain paper this size to use as a pattern. The binding must have the title and name of the author on its front cover, and this must therefore be either printed, block printed or drawn on the covering material. This may be transferred from the old cover or original letters may be used. A block printed cover makes an attractive binding. Take the pattern and rule it as shown in Fig. 3. This will make the locating of the front cover quite simple. Note that the lettering appears on the right hand side of the material when its finished side is up. This is shown in Fig. 1. Draw in the title and name on the pattern, so that perfection can be obtained before transferring it to the covering material.

Fig. 1   Fig. 2

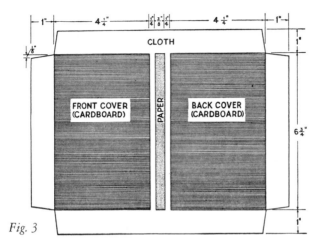

Front cover labels: **FRONT COVER (CARDBOARD)**, **PAPER**, **BACK COVER (CARDBOARD)**, **CLOTH**

Dimensions: 1", 4 ¼", ¼" ¼" ⅛", 4 ¼", 1", ⅛", 1", 6 ¾", 1"

Fig. 3

Step 4. Cut the covering material to size with the aid of the pattern. Cloth, if used, should be ironed and placed with finished side up on a flat surface. Locate the correct position for the lettering by placing the pattern over the cloth. Shade the back of the pattern with pencil marks and retrace over your original lines. Remove the pattern and finish the printing on the material, as shown in Fig. 1.

Step 5. Two cardboard covers and a paper back are now cut to size. For a small book of this nature the cardboard need not be over ¹⁄₁₆-inch in thickness, so if binder's board can be obtained you will want a sheet of .060" size. From this cut two covers for the binder. For the book chosen here, each must be 4¼-inch wide and 6¾-inch long, as shown in Fig. 3. The back can be cut from an ordinary piece of typewriter paper. This will be the length of the covers and the exact thickness of the filler in width. Place these three pieces on your pattern and test them for correct size.

Step 6. The covers and back are now pasted in position on the covering material. Lay the material on a flat surface with its wrong side up and the half having the lettering on the left as shown in Fig. 2. Measure 1 inch from the top and bottom of the cloth in its exact center. If the pattern will show through the cloth, it is best to place the material on the pattern, hold it down with pins, and paste the back strip and covers directly over their locations showing through. This back strip must be parallel with the sides of the material and 1 inch in from its top and bottom edges. The front and back cardboards are now coated with the paste and pressed down on the cloth in their correct positions. Note that these are located on each side of the back strip with their edges ¼-inch apart. See that the ends of all three pieces are on a line with each other. Press with weights until dry. If properly done, the three pieces will appear exactly as shown in Fig. 3.

Step 7. When dry, the corners of the material are cut away as shown in Fig. 3. Note that these are not cut at right angles, but ⅛-inch beyond. This insures against possible overlapping of the material. Turn these corners over and carefully crease the material along the edges of the cardboards and back strip. Coat with the paste and press in place. Allow to dry thoroughly under weights. Note this operation completed in Fig. 4.

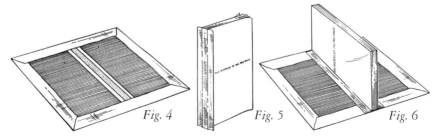

Fig. 4   *Fig. 5*   *Fig. 6*

Step 8. The filler is now prepared for the covers. This is done by attaching the cloth hinge to the filler's back, as shown in Fig. 5. Cut a strip of the buckram or any material you have chosen to use to size. The width will be the thickness of the filler plus 1 inch, while its length will be the length of the filler. Lay the strip flat on the table and coat the back of the filler with paste. Place the filler on the buckram so that is exactly centered on the cloth. Test to see that the cloth extends out on both sides from the filler. The top and bottom of the cloth and filler must be flush with each other. If loose threads appear along the back of the filler, do not remove them, as these tend to strengthen the binding between the buckram and the filler. The flaps which extend out on each side of the filler are left free, as shown in Fig. 5.

Step 9. The filler is now mounted within the covers. Before this can be done, the buckram on the filler should be given plenty of time to thoroughly dry. Lay the binder on a flat surface with the wrong side up, as shown in Fig. 6. See that the front cover with its printing is on the left side with the printing as in Fig. 2. Place the filler squarely on the center paper strip of the binder, so that the top and bottom of the binder extend beyond the filler an equal distance of ⅛-inch. See that the printed text and the printed cover read the same way. Do not make the mistake

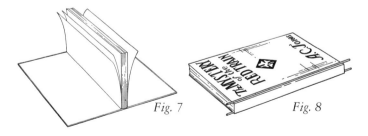

Fig. 7

Fig. 8

of placing your filler in its binder so that the text of the filler will be upside-down when its title is not. When the filler is in this position, as shown in Fig. 6, the extending back flaps are pasted to the cardboard covers. Do not paste the back of the filler to the center paper strip, but only the free buckram flaps.

Place other books on either side of the filler tight against it and over the flaps until dry. This assembly should appear as shown in Fig. 6. Give it plenty of drying time.

Step 10. Lining papers are now cut and pasted in place. Obtain the exact measurements of a page of the book. Two pieces of lining paper are cut the exact length of the page and twice its width. For the book illustrated here, these measurements would be 6¾-inch long and 8½-inch wide, or the width of two pages. Choose a color of the same tone as your covering material, or use an attractively designed paper. This is now trimmed to fit the cover. This piece not only covers the inside of the cover, but it also serves as a page in the finished book. The half which is to be pasted as a lining for the cover must be ⅛-inch smaller on top, bottom and outer side than the cover, while the other half remains the exact size of the pages of the book. After trimming, test each piece to see that the one side is properly cut to fit the cover while the other matches the filler pages. Coat the inside of one cover with paste, place the lining paper in position on it, and press until dry. The other half of the paper is left free. When the paste has dried, a ¼-inch wide strip along the crease forming the lining half and the fly-leaf is coated with paste. This coated strip is now pressed in place along the first page of the filler. The same procedure is used for the other cover. Pasting a narrow strip of the front lining paper to the first page and the back lining paper to the last page in this manner hides the cloth hinge and strengthens the joint of the cover. Note these lining papers in Fig. 7.

Step 11. The book is now pressed. To do this, place several sheets of paper between the covers and the first and last pages of the book. Close the book and place two long knitting needles, lengths of heavy wire, ice picks, or wood match sticks laid in a row, in the grooves formed by the covers and the back of the book when closed. Note this assembly in Fig. 8. When in this position, place several heavy books on the top cover and allow the assembly to dry. The extra sheets of paper prevent the paste from penetrating into the book and possible warping it. This completes the binding.

✤ LOOSE-LEAF BINDER ✤

Loose-leaf binders are made in much the same manner as the binding of a book. In the case of this type of binder, each cover is made separately with no back. The covers are lined with covering material, which is hidden on the inside face with a lining paper. No fly-leaf paper is used. Each cover has a hinge strip much like the back strip of the book. This is attached with buckram before the inner lining paper is pasted in place. Both covers are then pierced for binding cord. A shoe lace makes a splendid one. Binding tubes are usually used to prevent the cord from tearing the inserts.

✤ SCRAPBOOKS AND PHOTO ALBUMS ✤

Materials needed to make a durable scrapbook or photo album are as follows: 50 sheets craft paper, 15 by 18 inches; 50 strips craft paper, 2 by 18-½ inches; 1 spool heavy linen thread; ½ pt. best liquid glue; 2 pieces of wood 18-⅔ by 2 inches. While these are the recommended materials, anything suitable can be substituted, such as heavy wrapping paper, cardboard, or cloth instead of canvas. If canvas is used, the cover can be made more attractive if it is dyed a bright color. Also, the size of the scrapbook can be varied to suit your requirements.

To begin, drill the strips of wood to the dimensions shown in Fig. 10 and clamp them on the edges of the paper sheets of the album so that the strips extend ¼-inch beyond the paper at either end, as in Fig. 9. Using a ³⁄₁₆-inch bit, drill the sheets and also the strips of paper. Insert ³⁄₁₆-inch dowels, 6-inch long, in each end hole of one of the wooden strips.

Then place four of the large sheets and then four of the paper strips over the pins and continue placing the paper and strips in groups of four each.

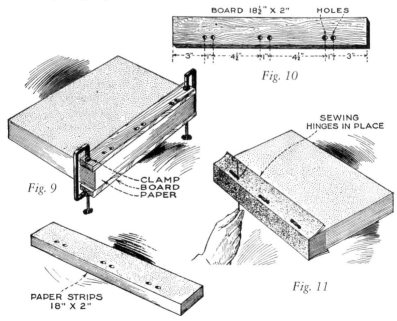

BOARD 18½" X 2"   HOLES

|← 3" →|←1"→|←— 4½" —|←1"→|←—— 4½" ——|←1"→|← 3" →|

Fig. 10

Fig. 9

CLAMP
BOARD
PAPER

PAPER STRIPS
18" X 2"

SEWING
HINGES IN PLACE

Fig. 11

In the finished book the strips compensate for thick items in the collection and can be used to glue in extra sheets if needed. Next, remove the dowels and clamp the other wooden strip on the paper assembly so that all drilled holes are in line. Then fill the holes with glue.

After the glue has dried for at least 12 hours, remove the clamps and drill through the hardened glue with an ⅛-inch bit, which leaves some of the glue still in the holes. The smaller piece of canvas is cut into two 6-inch strips, which are glued onto the back of the book to serve as hinges. Additional reinforcement is provided by stitching through the holes as in Fig. 11, with as many stitches as can be taken. A heavy darning needle and a 16-ft. length of thread, doubled twice to make a thread of four strands about 4 ft. long, are used for the sewing. Insert one of the binding boards between the hinges so that it extends about ½-inch beyond the side and ends of the pages. Pencil a guide line on the binding board to indicate where the edge of the hinge comes. Then remove the board from the hinge, and coat the inside surfaces of the hinge with hot glue, using waxed paper to protect the inside pages from the glue. After this the binding board is replaced in the hinge. When both binding boards are attached, and the glue has dried, apply the canvas cover and the inside end papers to the binding boards.

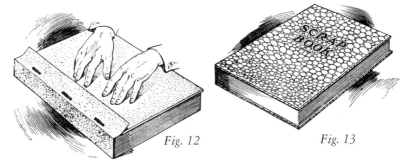

Fig. 12 *Fig. 13*

BLOCK PRINTING

Block Printing is a method by which permanent designs are transferred to various surfaces. The design is carved on a wood or linoleum block, inked with the desired color, and then pressed in place on the surface being decorated. This method of printing is another of the crafts traceable directly to China where it was known and practiced as early as the T'ang dynasty (A.D. 618–905).

Linoleum was introduced in America as a substitute for wood, in 1910. It had been used previously for some time in Europe. It was found that the linoleum block had many advantages over wood, as it is void of grain, will not splinter, and is far easier to carve. While the linoleum will not stand up under as many printings as the wood, it easily withstands the general usage demanded by the amateur. When a linoleum block is used in place of wood, the craft is often referred to as "lino-block" printing, although the actual process remains the same.

It will be found ideal for any type of decorative multiple printing where the design is to be repeated a number of times. Its greatest use is for the printing of holiday, announcement and place cards, the making of personal stationery, book plates and covers, wall hangings, table covers, insignia, curtains, etc. Christmas, Easter, Hallowe'en, Valentine, and Birthday cards, when block printed, reflect the individuality in thought and effort of the sender in a way no commercial card could ever do. The market for such cards, stationery, book plates, etc., is an ever growing one throughout the world today.

So that the reader will find a personal use as well as a ready market for the instruction project he creates from this booklet, the printing of stationery has been chosen as an example of the basic principles of this craft. While the insignia of the 98th Division has been chosen for illustrative purposes, the reader should substitute his own insignia when actually doing the work. In this manner, he will not only be able to use his own stationery, but should also find a ready market among his outfit for its sale.

Complete step-by-step instructions are given here for the completion of this work. If these are followed carefully, the worker will learn the basic principles of block printing which will lead toward mastery of the craft.

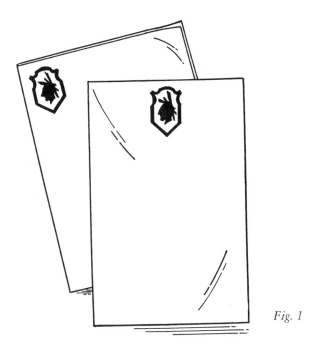

Fig. 1

✦ TOOLS AND MATERIALS ✦

Linoleum Carvers. Cutters are made especially for carving linoleum. They resemble pens, usually numbered to indicate shapes, and the five most popular of these are shown in Fig. 3. They are kept sharp with the aid of a small hand stone. While the five shown here do not by any means make up a complete set, they will be found sufficient for the general type of carving the amateur will wish to do. The first three shapes are known as "veiners," while the last two are called "gouges." The former are used to fine line work and the gouges for heavy lines and routing work.

Brayer. A brayer, or ink roller, is used to spread the ink evenly on the block. Such a tool is shown in Figs. 6 and 7. The ink is squeezed from the tube on a slab of marble or piece of glass and is distributed evenly over the glass until a thin film results, as shown in Fig. 6. Roll the brayer in all directions until the ink covers the roller in a thin film. If a brayer is not available, a common rolling pin wrapped in ordinary gauze can be substituted.

Linoleum Block. Linoleum cut to desired size in the shape of blocks is used for this type of printing. The required size of the design determines the size of the block. A cork-filled, unglazed, battleship-gray linoleum of about ¼-inch thickness is recommended. Linoleum blocks are of two types, the mounted and the unmounted. The former has the linoleum glued to a plywood block, and is used with a press or when the printing is to be done on paper. The latter is left without the wood backing for printing on cloth. For instruction purposes in this book a mounted block is used, as shown in Fig. 5.

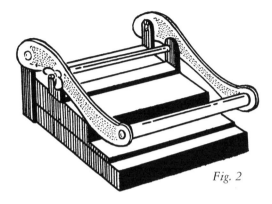

Fig. 2

Inks. For paper and cardboard printing, the new watercolor inks are highly recommended, as they blend well and permit the cleaning of the block, brayer, and glass with water. For fast color printing on cloth, printer's half-tone inks should be used. Tubes are recommended. Red, blue, black, and yellow should be kept on hand.

Paper. Any good, soft-textured paper, such as the handmade, mimeograph, rice, or second-copy typing bonds, are suitable for this work, as they will absorb the ink and dry quickly. Use white or the lighter shades, such as light green, gray, blue, or other pastel colors.

Fig. 3

✤ BLOCK-PRINTED STATIONERY ✤

Step 1. The first requirement of this craft is the selection of the design. In the illustrations in this book, the insignia of the 98th Division has been arbitrarily chosen merely for its instructional purposes. To make your work popular, it is suggested that the insignia of your own outfit be substituted for the one shown. If possible, obtain a picture of your shoulder patch and rule it with the same number of squares shown in Fig. 4. Those may be any size. Now rule a thin sheet of paper with ¼-inch squares of the same total number, and make a copy of the insignia on this paper. Such a drawing is known as a "graph." When making such a drawing, see that the line you are drawing on your ruled paper passes through each square in exactly the same location the corresponding line passes through the same squares of the graph plan. By making the copy square by square, the work of freehand drawing becomes considerably simplified.

Step 2. Note that the head of the Indian turns toward the right instead of the left. This is actually backward, so that when the design is turned over on the paper and printed the insignia will appear correct. In other words, all blocks must be carved in reverse, and for this reason all patterns must be copied in the same way whenever possible. However, if the design is being drawn freehand from a graphed plan, it will be easier to do so in the usual way on thin paper. The penciled tracing is then turned over on the block of linoleum and a pencil traced over the original lines showing through to the back. If the drawing is too thin to show through to the back, a piece of carbon paper may be placed under it with the carbon side up. The lines are then reversed and the carbon will transfer the drawing in reverse on the back.

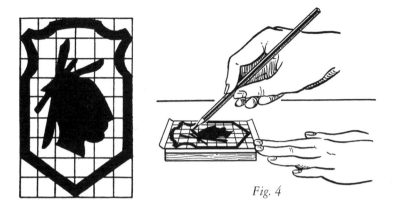

Fig. 4

Step 3. Cut a piece of linoleum approximately 1 ¾-inch wide and 2 ½-inch long. Glue the back of the linoleum piece to a block of wood the same size. If you should have mounted blocks this will not be not necessary.

Step 4. The pattern is now centered on the block in reverse and the design transferred to it by tracing over its lines with a sharp pencil, as shown in Fig. 4. It will be noted in this figure that the design has been showed "filled in" with block printing ink. This is done for clarity, although some advocate this step as a safeguard against errors in copying and cutting. It also serves to give a picture of the finished design to the worker. When the tracing has been completed on the linoleum block, the design and its border, if it has one, should be carefully filled in with the ink as a guide to the worker. All such filled-in areas will be left in relief, or untouched by the knife, as showed in Fig. 5. Only these parts will be printed on the paper.

Step 5. The block is now carved. For all fine lines and similar details, the carver is held in the hand like a pen or pencil, which is shown at the bottom right of Fig. 5. For heavy lines and routing out large areas, it should be held with the handle cupped in the palm with the forefinger guiding it. Keep from "digging in" over the cutting edge of the tool, as this results in "breaking" or ragged lines. The proper sloping edge is shown at top of Fig. 5, "Right." The edges show as "Wrong" result in blurred edges which often break with printing. This is also shown in Fig. 5 at the bottom left. Take your time, follow each line carefully, see that your cuts are deep enough to insure against printing, watch your shoulder cuts to see that they are beveled, as shown, and keep your cutters sharp.

Step 6. The ink is now prepared. Squeeze a slight amount of the ink in the desired color on the glass, after the glass has been carefully wiped clean. With the brayer, distribute it evenly over the glass until a thin film on the brayer results, as shown in Fig. 6.

Step 7. Lay the linoleum block on a flat surface, such as the table or bench, with its carved design facing up. Hold it in place and carefully roll the brayer over the surface of the block in all directions until it becomes well inked, as shown in Fig. 7.

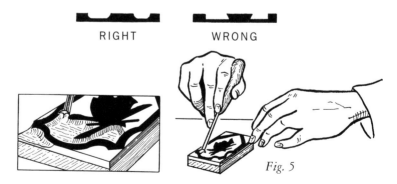

RIGHT   WRONG

Fig. 5

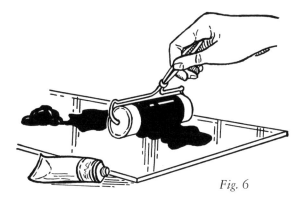

Fig. 6

Step 8. A "proof" of the block is now taken on scrap material. When doing this always use the same material, such as the paper you are printing on for the finished stationery, so that results may be correctly read. If the proof should prove unclear, it indicates either lack of pressure on the block in printing or not enough ink on the block. If blotchy, the block has too much ink or it has not been carved deeply enough. Correct either the block or the inking, as the case may be, and continue taking proofs of the printing until perfect results are obtained.

Step 9. A popular hand press is shown in Fig. 2. Before actual printing of the stationery is started, study the two positions of the emblem shown in Fig. 1. Some prefer the insignia centered at the top, while others wish it at the side. In either case, care must be taken to see that the printing block is perfectly in line with the side and top of the paper. Slip a piece of the paper onto the press bed, place the block on the paper in the position desired, and apply pressure. The amount of pressure required is controlled by the amount of solid area in the cut. As the area increases, the pressure must increase. Thus, if the emblem is made up of fine line-work on cut-out areas, less pressure is

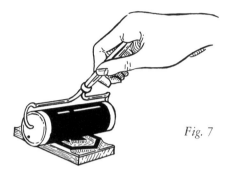

Fig. 7

required. Make a number of practice printings and you will soon be able to judge the exact amount of pressure required. Never allow wet prints to contact each other. Keep re-inking the block as the paper is printed. This completes single-color printing.

✢ COLOR PRINTING ✢

A few words on the process of color-printing may help the novice to understand its principles. The process is much the same as single-color except that each color must have its own block carved for it. As an example, let us say we wish to print a house in color. The house is to be one color, while its door is to be of another. A block of the house is carved with its door cut away so that it will not print. This is then printed in the desired color. A second block is then carved with nothing but the door in relief. This is in turn inked with another color and printed over the first print. The art in color printing lies to a great extent in placing the blocks in exactly the correct position on the surface being printed. It is not simple by any means, but practiced repetition cannot fail to bring success.

ZZZ: Monogram alphabet

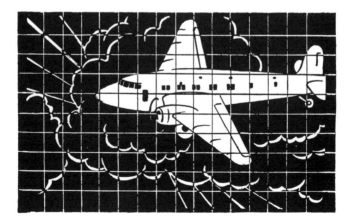

❖ MISCELLANEOUS DESIGNS ❖

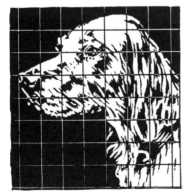

AXE CRAFT

In the days of our forefathers the axe was the most important tool known. It alone often formed the entire tool chest of the Pilgrims. With it this country was originally built. Forests were cleared, forts were erected, houses built, heat provided, fences made, furniture constructed and living made possible through the use of this tool so representative of American life. In our modern life of today we find axe-craft almost a lost art, although in our great reserves, our mountains and forest country we find life flowing on in much the same manner as it did when our ancestors hewed from these lands the foundations for our great cities of today.

With the passing of time and the perfection of manufacture, the attraction of hewed articles returns as a constant reminder of our origin, and their popularity increases as a form of "early American" never to be forgotten. The creation of such articles is not by any means a crowded field, and we find rustic furniture ever in demand by our large stores for both garden and porch use. It not only permits the craftsman to make his own articles, but anyone—handy with their axe—finds a ready market for the articles he builds.

While most of the booklets of this series contain step-by-step instructions for finishing one or more articles in a craft, as a means of teaching basic principles, such a procedure is not of value in this particular type of work. It is more important that the novice learn the proper method of handling the axe together with the construction of the most useful type of joints. When this has been accomplished, it becomes a matter of choosing the articles he wishes to build and obtaining attractive designs for them. This booklet gives data on the handling and care of the axe, the construction of joints, and a good number of different types of articles easily made. The imagination and ingenuity of the worker are the deciding factors of his progress once he has mastered his axe, its care, and basic construction methods.

✦ TOOLS AND MATERIALS ✦

The Axe. The true woodsman has great respect but no fear for his axe. It is no more dangerous than any other sharp-edged tool, but as such it must be handled carefully and in the proper manner. Its correct use is an art in itself, and the chopping of wood is far more than the mere hitting of it with an axe. Learn to use it properly and even the beginner will be surprised and delighted with the work he can do. Get a good one, keep it sharp and learn to use it correctly. Here are a few "safety-first" hints:

1. *Obtain the best.* Cheap handles that break and heads that fly off are dangerous things.

2. *Keep it sharp.* Dull edges cause glancing blows and these in turn cause the large majority of accidents that occur with axes.

3. *Do not crowd your work.* Keep clear with a free striking distance. If this is practiced, hands, knees and feet will never be in the path of your blade.

4. *Clear a space around you.* Clear a space equal to the distance of the axe when held at full arm's length. Hold the axe out in this manner and clear a circle of this size around you. Remove all vines, sticks, brush, etc., within this circle before starting work, so that nothing can deflect your axe.

5. *Look behind you.* Make sure that no one is standing directly behind you when starting a stroke. The upswinging axe could cause great harm to another should it strike him.

To hold the axe properly, grasp it firmly in the hand near the end of the handle, as shown in Fig. 1 "A." This is much the same as the hold on a hammer. The safest method of splitting boards and small logs is shown at "E." This should be practiced by beginners. Place a log between you and the wood to be split. Lean the piece against the log on its far side with its end extending above the side of the log. In this way, any misdirected or

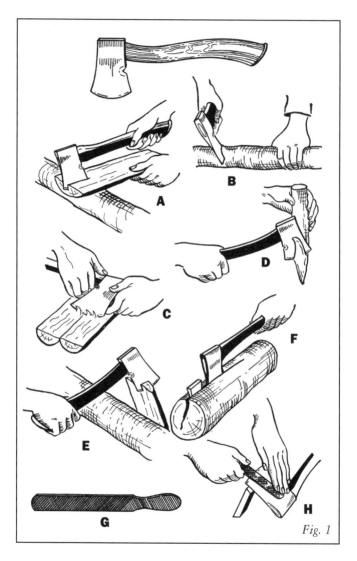

Fig. 1

glancing blows will fall harmlessly on the log. Split the wood by burying the axe blade in the end of the wood, as shown.

When more skill has been obtained, such wood can be split as shown at "A." Here, the end of the wood is placed on a firm log while the other end is held in the hand. When the axe strikes the board, it will not jump, as the log forms a firm base. When wood is split in this manner, it is struck on the face near the end, as shown. Fig "B" shows the correct way to cut a log. Never strike the log straight on, as this merely dulls the blade edge and makes the chopping more difficult. Drive the axe into the wood at an angle. In this way you are cutting nearer the direction of the grain, which gives deeper and faster cuts with considerably less effort. Keep the holding hand well away from the line of the axe stroke and hold the piece firmly.

Axe "planning," or smoothing, is shown at "C." In this work, the axe head is held in one hand while its handle is held in the other, as shown. The axe is used as a knife and the action is one of shaving rather than cutting. Table tops, chair bottoms, and other surfaces requiring smoothing can be finished in this manner. The blade must be extremely sharp and all shaving must be done with the grain of the wood.

When cutting socket joints, as shown in Fig. 2 at "D," or other stakes requiring a sharp point, hold the stake as shown in Fig. 1 at "D." The end being sharpened should rest on a flat surface, such as a half log, so that the force of the blow will not drive it into the ground. Slowly work around the stake until all sides have been cut. This is considerably like sharpening a pencil with a knife.

Splitting logs for table tops, seats, etc., is usually considered the hardest job of the woodsman, but with practice the amateur will experience little trouble. For large log splitting, a maul and iron wedges will be necessary, but for the size logs required for this work the axe and a wood wedge will serve, as shown at "F."

Study the log carefully so that all splitting will be done with the grain. Place the log on a level stretch of ground, and drive the axe into the end of the log in its center. Remove the axe and drive it into the log again just above this first cut, but on the side of the log. While the axe is still in the log, place a wedge in the crack opened up by this second blow. Remove the axe and drive the wedge in deeper. Continue the cuts down the center side of the log, moving the wedge each time and driving it deeper into the log. When splitting logs, give the axe a twisting motion to open the cut and keep the axe from sticking. If the log is particularly long, two or more wedges should be used, which can be cut in the same manner as the stake at "D."

The File. A first-class axe, properly used, should never need a grindstone. An axe file, such as shown at "G," will keep the axe in proper condition. Such files have a coarse, fast-cutting surface on one side and a smooth, finishing surface on the other. Get the habit of sharpening your axe often with the file, and it will be in good condition at all times for all work. The best method of sharpening the axe is shown at "H." Drive a small stake into the ground and rest the blade of the axe against it, as shown. Hold the file level with the blade and file only on the forward stroke, lifting it clear on the return stroke. With the rough side of the file, file the flat of the blade ½-inch from the edge. From this line, file the flat away to a line about three inches back from the edge. Do not file further back than this, as it will cause your axe to stick or possibly break. When the flat of the blade has been filed, the bevel is sharpened with the smooth surface of the file. When this is completed, go over the flat of the blade with the smooth side of the file to remove any roughness. Always file the axe in this manner. If the flat of the blade is not filed and then followed by the filing of the bevel, the blade will soon become stubby, and the axe will not sink in the wood. The proportionate thinness of the blade and the bevel must be kept at all times, so both must be filed together in this manner.

✥ JOINTS ✥

Cross Lap. This type of joint is used where two logs must cross each other and at the same time have their top and bottom surfaces flush. It is shown before assembly in Fig. 2 at "A." Such joints are used where cross members, such as leg supports under tables, chairs, and benches, require additional strength and firmness in the joint. An example of this may be seen in Fig. 6 at "A." To make such a joint, the logs are cut to exact length, crossed one on the other in the required position, carefully marked on each log where they cross, separated, and the cuts then made. The cut portions should be half the diameter of the log, but before the full depth is cut both should be tested in position constantly to make sure that the cuts fit each other and are not too deep. Then nail or bind.

Mitre. This joint is used for assembly of two butt ends of logs at an angle, such as on picture frames, casings, edgings, moldings, etc., as shown in Fig. 2 at "B." Typical examples can be seen in Fig. 4 at "C" and Fig. 7 at "C." To make such a joint, place the logs in the desired position with one on top of the other. Mark the angle on both logs while in position. The cuts are now made. While cutting, constantly test them together to insure correct angle. Such a joint is usually joined by driving nails through the side of one log into the mitred end of the other. This process is then reversed for added strength.

Bound Cross Lap. Such a joint, as shown in Fig. 2 at "C," may be made in three different ways. It is used for the same purposes as

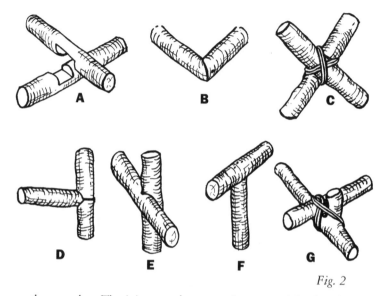

Fig. 2

the cross lap. The joint may be a cross lap, as explained under "Cross Lap," and then bound with cord, wire, leather thongs, or bark strippings. If so, its construction is exactly the same as the cross lap. The second method is a semi-cross, as shown at "G." The construction of these last two is explained under their own headings. Such joints are usually firmly nailed and then the wrapping used to both reinforce and hide the nails.

Open Mortise. Where the end of one log must butt against the side of the other in a joint requiring strength, this type is far superior to any other. It is shown in Fig. 2 at "D." The butt end of one log is cut in the form of a wedge, while the side of the other log is notched to take the wedge end of the first. The notch is cut to a depth of half the diameter of the log, while the wedge is cut with sides the same length as the sides of the notch. Cut the notch first. Now cut the wedge. When cutting the wedge keep testing it in the notch until a perfect fit results. Place the wedge in the notch, and drive a nail through the side of the notched log into the end of the wedged log.

Semi-cross Lap. This joint is shown in Fig. 2 at "E." It is used for the same general purposes as the cross lap, except that its logs are not flush with each other and it is not as strong or as firm a joint. It is constructed in exactly the same manner but in this case the depth of the cuts are a fourth of the logs' diameter while those of the cross lap are a full half. Such a joint is usually nailed and may also be reinforced by binding, as shown at "C."

Butt. This is the most common of all joints. It is used widely in rough log construction, where appearance, strength, and finish are not required. Such a joint is nothing more than the end of one log placed in position against the end or side of another, and the two firmly nailed together as shown at "F." Binding is not practical on such a joint. Shape the end of the log to conform with the side of its joining one to secure a good fit.

Forked Cross. Forked cross joints are widely used in all types of rustic log construction. The primitive appearance adds greatly to the realistic charm of axe-craft furniture. Such a joint is shown in Fig. 2 at "G." A forked log is cut with the fork trimmed slightly longer than the diameter of the log it is to hold. The second log is then placed in the fork, nailed securely, and the joint carefully bound, as shown.

While the worker will develop a great many more joints as he progresses in his work, those given above will serve for all general purposes.

✢ CONSTRUCTION OF ARTICLES ✢

This type of construction does not permit step-by-step details being given. The worker will find that a careful study of the illustrations of the finished articles will be sufficient to carry on the work.

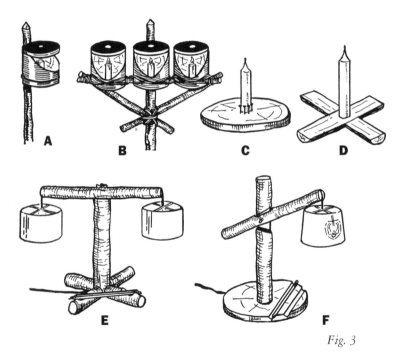

Fig. 3

Lighting Fixtures. A great variety of different light fixtures can be made most attractively in rustic construction. Those shown in Fig. 3 and Fig. 6 give enough details to permit the beginner to either make these or design his own. The single lamp at

"A" is merely a tin can with a hole cut in the top, half the can side cut away, and then mounted on a pole. At "B" a candelabra type of the same lamp is mounted. Two forms of simple candlesticks are shown at "C" and "D." The desk lamps shown at "E" and "F" are simply built of logs. The one at "F" is adjustable, having a butterfly nut to hold the shade rod.

Picture and Mirror Frames. Four types of frames are shown in Fig. 4. These are all grooved on half logs at the back to take the mirror or picture and glass. The one at "A" is made of four half logs, grooved at the back, and put together with a cross lap joint at each corner, as shown in Fig. 2 at "A." The frame at "B" is made of small, short logs mounted on thin backing. These are mitred at the corners and glued in place. A common type of frame is shown at "C," which consists of nothing more than four half logs, mitred at the joints, and grooved to take the glass and picture. A mitred joint is shown at "B" in Fig. 2. A butt joint frame is shown in Fig. 4 at "D." This is made of four half logs, grooved along their backs, and butt jointed to each other. A butt joint is shown at "F" of Fig. 2.

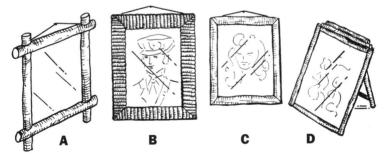

Fig. 4

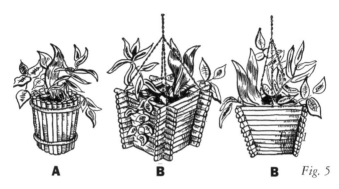

A **B** **B** *Fig. 5*

Plant Baskets. Three types of plant holders are shown in Fig. 5. The one at "A" is a floor or table type, while those at "B" and "C" are hanging baskets. Normal "stockade" construction is used at "A," and those at "B" and "C" are of "log cabin" design. The last two have their logs notched to fit tightly one on top of the other.

Ceiling Fixtures. There is no end to the number of designs one can make in ceiling lighting fixtures. Two are shown in Fig. 6 at "A" and "B." Those are made of full logs with the wires running along the sides or tops to conceal them from below.

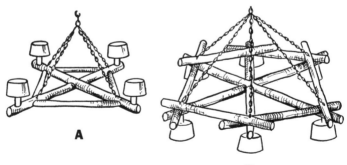

A

B *Fig. 6*

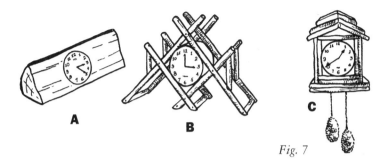

Fig. 7

Clocks. In Fig. 7 at "A" and "B" two types of mantle clocks are shown, while a cuckoo clock for hanging on the wall is shown at "C." All these are ordinary round clocks mounted in log bases. The cuckoo clock is a round clock mounted in a box, which in turn is dressed with logs to carry out the idea of the real cuckoo construction. Pine cones are used to fake the winding "weights."

Bird Houses. Any number of bird houses can be made of rustic work. Three unique ones are shown in Fig. 8 at "A," "B," and "C." The one at "A" is a double house of cuckoo clock construction, while the second one at "B" is a replica of the log cabin. The last one at "C" is a hollow log roofed with logs.

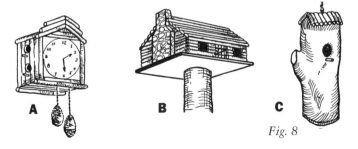

Fig. 8

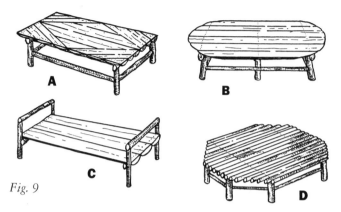

Fig. 9

Coffee Tables. Four types of coffee tables are shown in Fig. 9. These introduce two types of top construction, the full log and the half log. If full logs are to be used, they should be not over 1 inch in diameter and closely fitted together. Half logs are usually mounted with under braces, and then axe shaved or planed smooth.

Tables. All types, shapes, and sizes of tables are possible in log work. The five shown in Fig. 10 give an idea of construction and design. All have half log top construction with the usual under bracing on legs. The one shown at "A" is splendid for outdoor dining, while the eight-sided one at "B" makes a good card table. One of the most attractive designs is shown at "C," while the mitred joints of the table at "D" add to its unique charm. Another type of dining table is shown at "E."

Chairs and Settees. In Fig. 11 seven types of chair design are shown, as well as a combination settee and table and a single love seat. The camp chair at "A" is made for a canvas seat, while the straight chairs at "B," "C," and "D" are fine for the dinner

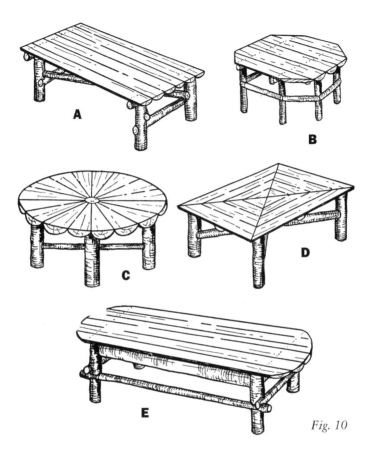

Fig. 10

table. The large combination at "E" is made to take a single bed mattress on the seat and a second one at the back. These should be attractively covered in some bright material. The small love seat is merely a suggestion for the builder to follow with his own designs. The other three chairs at "G," "H," and "I" are arm chairs for the garden or game room.

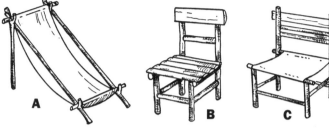

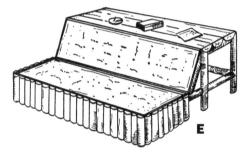

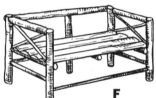

Fig. 11

Outdoor Diner. This combination bench and table is quite as good indoors as out, and is most popular in the permanent camp, cabin dining room, or the game room. It is shown at Fig. 12 at "A."

Stools. All kinds of stools can be easily constructed of logs. The one shown in Fig. 12 at "B" is made for a canvas top, while those at "C" and "D" have wood tops. The one at "C" is of slab seat make, while the other is of split logs. The high stool at "E" belongs in the bar.

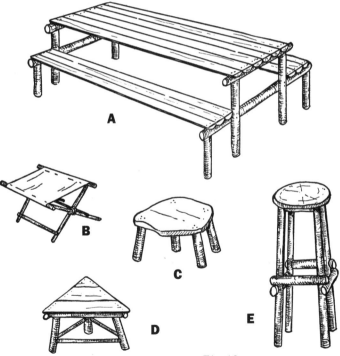

Fig. 12

TIN-CAN-CRAFT

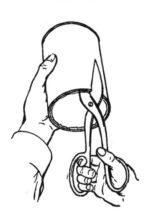

Tin-can-craft, as its name implies, is the making of useful and attractive articles from used tin cans. It is a craft originated and developed as a substitute for art metalcraft. As the latter requires expensive and often unobtainable metals, such as pewter, brass, copper, silver, or gold, it becomes evident that a material must be found to replace them. Tin is a natural substitute and long experimentation has proved that while the same methods may not in all cases be followed, the same results can be obtained. Almost all articles created in the finer metals can be made quite as beautiful in tin.

For clarity, tin-can-craft can be divided into two major groups. The first of these, which will be covered by this book, is the simple type of work requiring none of the more difficult steps such as plating, soldering, heat treating, or stone setting. To this group belong such articles as flower pots, door stops, book ends, pad holders, candlesticks, nut, fruit, and flower bowls. The second includes every known type of work done in any metal. Such articles as fine jewelry, vases, boxes, trays, letter knives, desk sets, lanterns, and other artistically wrought items of like nature may be created.

The basic principles of tin-can-craft are fully explained in this book by giving the step-by-step methods of making a candlestick. This is created with the least amount of inexpensive tools and requires no knowledge or experience of the worker. However, if each step is followed closely the beginner will have no difficulty in mastering the basic methods of tin-can-craft construction, which will form a good foundation for future work.

No difficulty will be found in locating materials required. This ranges from tiny caviar tins to five gallon drums. If possible, obtain your tins as they are opened, so that they can be thoroughly washed and carefully dried to prevent rusting. No mess sergeant on earth will do less than thank you for taking them away. So let's get to work, make our first project, and see why everyone thinks it is fascinating.

✤ TOOLS ✤

In Fig. 1 are shown all the tools necessary for completing simple tin-can-craft projects, such as the candlestick being used for instructional purposes. Each of these will be discussed in turn.

Straight Shears. The most useful tool you could have in your tin-can-craft kit is a pair of metal cutting shears or snips. A lightweight pair is recommended, as shown at "A."

Ball Pein Hammer. Such a hammer, often referred to as a "machinists' hammer," is sufficient for all general work. The rounded end, or ball pein, is used for planishing operations, as well as for rounding the heads of rivets. The flat head is for driving such tools as punches, chisels, etc. Such a hammer is shown in Fig. 1, "B."

Scriber. After designs or dimension lines have been traced on the tin plate, a scriber, or "scratch awl," is used to scratch them in for permanency. The one shown at "C" has a ⅞-inch diameter handle and a 2⅞-inch blade. An ice pick can be substituted for the scriber if one is not procurable.

Bending Block. This consists of a squared-up block of hard wood of any desired size. It is splendid for making straight bends in the tin. Such blocks should be cut to size as they are needed for each job, and if each one is kept, the worker will soon have a valuable set of varying sizes and shapes. Note the one at "D."

Ruler. While a wood rule can be used, a steel one will prove superior for tin plate work. A 12-inch rule with graduations in fractions is recommended, as shown at "E."

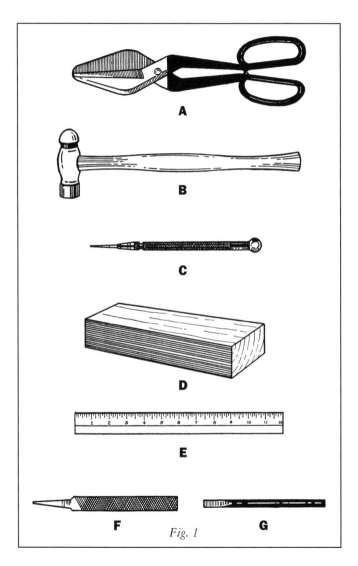

A

B

C

D

E

F   *Fig. 1*   G

File. A flat file is necessary to round and smooth edges left rough by the shears. Never work with tin plate until its edges have been filed smooth. Such a file is shown at "F."

Cold Chisel. The cold chisel, shown in Fig. 1, "G," is used with the hammer to cut inside areas, as illustrated in Fig. 6. A ¼-inch wide chisel is recommended for all general purposes where only one is being provided.

✤ CANDLESTICK ✤

This combination wall and table candle bracket of Colonial design should be made of fairly heavy tin, such as is found in gasoline, oil, or grease cans. Follow each step as it is given here and no difficulty will be had in completing this useful and attractive tin-can-craft article.

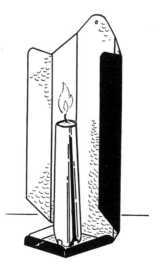

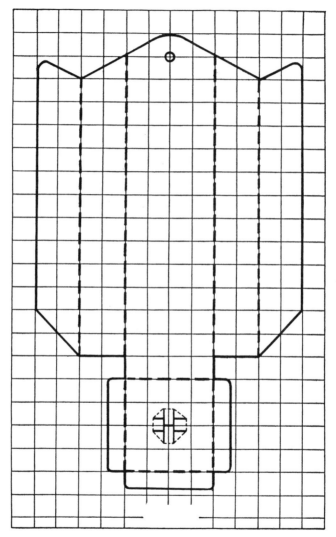

Fig. 2

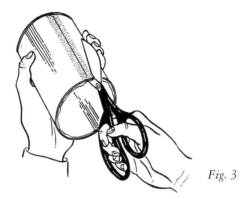

Fig. 3

Step 1. The pattern for the candle holder is shown in Fig. 2 on squares representing ½-inch each. This is known as a "graph plan" and will prove of great help whenever copy work is required. Rule a sheet of paper with ½-inch squares. With your pencil and ruler lay out the full-size pattern of the holder on this paper. When doing this, make sure that the line you are drawing on your sheet passes through each square in exactly the same position as the corresponding line of the graph plan passes through its squares.

Step 2. Obtain a tin can large enough to produce a piece of metal 6 inches wide and 10 inches long. Open out the can by shearing along both sides of its side seam, as shown in Fig. 3. Make these cuts from the open end to the closed bottom. Now shear around the bottom and open out the can. The top seam, if not already removed by opening, should be sheared away at this time. Bend the tin in the direction opposite to its natural curve until it lies flat.

Step 3. The pattern is now transferred to the tin plate. If the can once contained a greasy food or substance, it should be

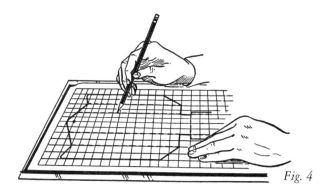

Fig. 4

thoroughly washed with soap and water, dried carefully, and then polished with a soft cloth. Place a sheet of carbon paper, shiny side down, on the tin with the pattern centered on the carbon. Carefully trace over all lines of the pattern with a sharp pencil, as shown in Fig. 4. Remove the carbon and pattern. Carefully retrace the pattern lines appearing on the tin with the scriber. Do this with great care.

Step 4. The outline of the holder is now cut out of the tin. Shear along the outer scribed lines. Do this carefully. Keep the guiding blade of the shears directly on the line being cut. Great care should be taken in handling the tin at this stage to prevent finger cuts from its ragged edges. It will be noted in Fig. 2 that the outer lines of the pattern appear solid while certain inner ones are shown dotted. The latter are lines on which the piece is bent but not cut.

Step 5. Any sheared or sawed edge of tin plate is dangerous to handle. While it appears smooth it is actually burred and bent in razor-sharp edges. For this reason all edges of tin plate should be filed carefully until smooth and round as early in the operation as possible. Do this now, as shown in Fig. 5. Filing should be done across the edge with a cross stroke, and also along the edge with an elongated stroke in the same manner as a knife is handled when whittling.

Step 6. The four small center flaps, which form the candle grip, are not cut with the chisel. Fig. 6 shows how this is done. Place the tin on a hard wood or steel block, as shown. Place the edge of the chisel directly on the line being cut with the chisel held vertically, and tap its handle with the hammer. Keep tapping until the cut is made through the tin plate. Cut only along the solid lines until four tabs result. These should not be bent at this time.

Step 7. The piece is now planished. This is a form of decoration given metal areas. It has long been used in the finest of art metalcraft articles. It produces the "hand-made" appearance so often considered a mark of distinction. Place the piece on a flat surface of hard wood or lead and softly tap its surface with the ball pein of the hammer. The entire surface is covered with the exception of the holder's base, which is left smooth. This results in a hammered texture which leaves the surface of the tin covered with glittering, brilliant facets. Never use the flat head of the hammer, as this might result in cuts and dents in the surface. Fig. 7 illustrates the correct procedure.

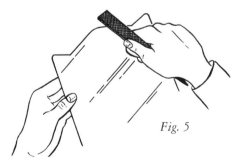

Fig. 5

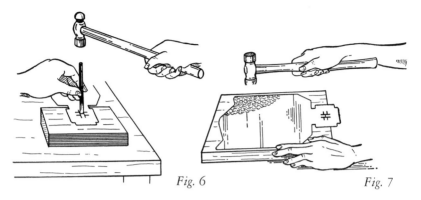

Fig. 6   Fig. 7

Step 8. The piece is now bent. Study the drawing of the finished holder. Note that the first bends are made along the longest inner dotted lines. These are bent at approximately 45° angles to the back, while the outer sections are bent at right angles to the back. Bend the inner sections first and then finish with the outer ones. To do this, a hard wood block should be cut 1-inch thick, 2 inches wide and at least 7 inches long. Place the block with its edge along the inner dotted line. Slowly push the tin up along the edge and then finish it to a sharp bend with the hammer. Note procedure shown in Fig. 8. The flat head of the hammer is carefully wrapped in cloth layers to prevent marring the tin surface. Always tap the metal lightly. A dozen light strokes are far better than one hard stroke. When the four long bends are completed, the four small center flaps of the base are bent up. Bend these at right angles with the base, and finish their edges by rounding and smoothing with the file. This is followed by bending the four sides of the base at right angles to the base. The base is then bent at right angles to the back, which completes the bending operation. Now go over the entire piece and make any adjustments necessary to see that the sides of the holder match perfectly. File the under side of the base to remove any burrs resulting from the chisel cuts of the center flaps. Test to see that the holder rests squarely on a flat surface.

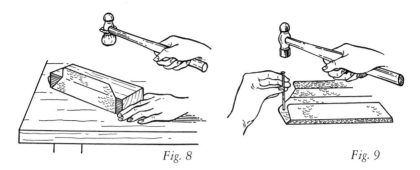

Fig. 8   *Fig. 9*

Step 9. Locate the exact center of the back at a point ½-inch from its top. To hang the holder on the wall a small hole is made at this point, as shown in Fig. 2. This can easily be done by driving an ordinary nail or spike through the tin, as shown in Fig. 9. File off any resulting burrs on the back.

Step 10. If the tin used for the candlestick is in good condition, an interesting finish can be given it by simply polishing the metal with a good metal polish, and then finishing it with clear varnish, lacquer, or white shellac to safeguard its polish. Another method of finishing such articles is with enamel, lacquer, or oil paint. Paint the inside white with the outer parts in any desired color. This completes your first tin-can-craft project.

❖ WHERE DO WE GO FROM HERE? ❖

While the candlestick was chosen as an interesting medium by which to show the primary principles of tin-can-craft and also because it might well prove of utilitarian value in any camp, post, or station, it is but one of hundreds of articles which can be made from used tin cans. Nothing but your lack of practice and imagination can limit you.

Every known type of work that has been possible to create in the finest of art metalcraft has been accomplished in tin. Nothing that can be done with pewter, brass, copper, silver, or gold has proved impossible with tin plate. Methods may differ but the results are the same.

Articles such as pad holders, thermometer brackets, candlesticks, bookends, nut, fruit, and flower bowls, doorstops, scoops, clips, tongs, trays, letter knives, ink wells, picture frames, monogram plates, lanterns, belt buckles, cuff links, vases, match and cigarette boxes, escutcheons, and ash trays are quickly, easily, and beautifully executed in tin plate. Why not go on from here, master this cheapest and most fascinating craft, and join the hundreds of others who have become expert tin-can-crafters?

✤ OTHER SUGGESTIONS ✤

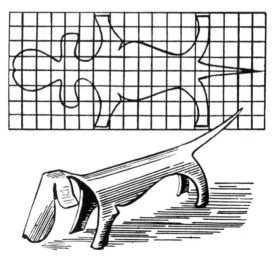

❖ NOVELTY ANIMAL SERVING TRAYS ❖

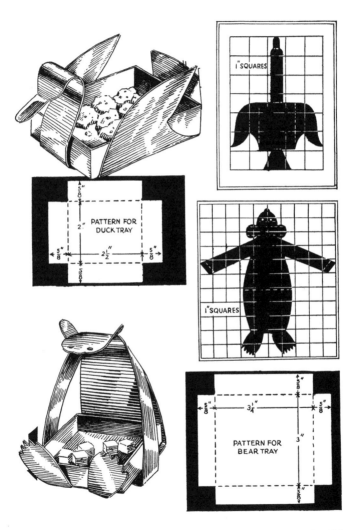

1" SQUARES

5/8"
5/8"
2"
PATTERN FOR
DUCK TRAY
5/8"
2 1/2"
5/8"
5/8"

1" SQUARES

5/8"
5/8"
3 1/4"
3"
PATTERN FOR
BEAR TRAY
5/8"

✤ FRAMED ART ✤

✣ DINNERWARE ✣

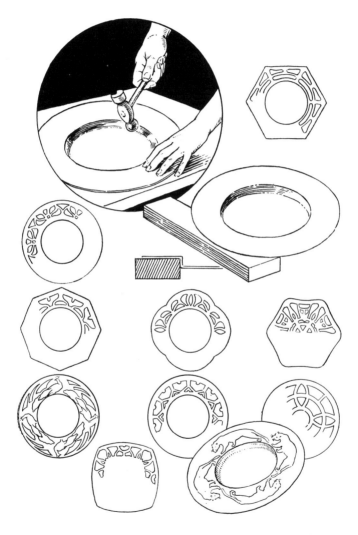

BRAIDING
AND
KNOTTING

Braiding and knotting is one of the most popular and enjoyable of all crafts. As a handicraft it provides a great deal of fun in making a variety of articles which are ornamental and useful. Both knotting and braiding have a great deal in common and certain principles when applied properly will enable you to produce many fine and worthwhile items. These include belts, bracelets, leashes, coasters, and purses.

❖ BRAIDING ❖

The round braid and the flat braid are identical in the procedure of making a lanyard (Fig. 1). For purposes of clarity the illustrations indicate the use of the flat braid although you will actually make the lanyard with a round braid.

Fig. 1

❖ HOW TO MAKE A LANYARD ❖

A very useful article you can make by braiding is a lanyard, an attractive cord to hold a whistle. This project needs little equipment or room. Before you begin to make your lanyard, here are some tips that will help you. Be sure to pull all strands tight and adjust the row of stitches. This will make the braid uniform and neat. If your strands get tangled, you can straighten them by holding the two left strands and pulling on the two at the right. If you must lay aside the braid before it is finished, keep the strands in place by using an ordinary paper clip on the loose strands, or tie them with a simple overhand knot. In following directions for making your lanyard, note the position for your hands and fingers in each step. Be sure that the strands are held tight and close to the last stitch at all times. Do not let the strands dangle loosely.

In making the lanyard you will use three different kinds of braid pattern: round braid, square braid, and Terminal Turk's Head. Start by using the round braid.

The materials you will need to make your lanyard are 2 different colored strands of pyro-cord, craftstrip, or similar material, each 3½-yards long; and 1 swivel snap (Fig. 2).

Now begin by drawing the two strands of your material evenly through the eye of the swivel snap. Hang your swivel snap firmly on a nail so that it will not slip while working. Arrange the strands as shown in the diagram, and counting from left to right, number the strands 1 to 4 (Fig. 3). Hold the center strands 2 and 3, with the forefinger and thumb of the right hand. Take strand 4 with the left hand (Fig. 4) and bring around the back to the left and forward to the front between strands 1 and 2 (Fig. 5).

Fig. 2

Fig. 3

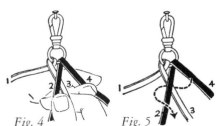

Fig. 4 *Fig. 5*

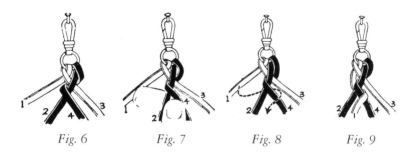

Fig. 6   Fig. 7   Fig. 8   Fig. 9

Fold over strand 2 so that it lies parallel to strand 3 (Fig. 6). Draw all the strands tight. Hold the center strands, 2 and 4, with the forefinger and thumb of the left hand. Take strand 1 with the right hand (Fig. 7) and forward to the front between strands 3 and 4 (Fig. 8). Draw all strands tight and continue braiding this way. If you make a mistake or become confused, take out 1 or 2 stitches so that the strands are back in a 2, 1, 4, 3 position as shown in the diagram (Fig. 9). Then follow the directions from step 3. The working strand, that is the one that is woven into the others, is always the uppermost outside strand on the right or left.

Continue the round braid until the strands are 12 inches long. End with an overhand knot. Hold the lanyard in the left hand and tie the two left strands over the two right strands (Fig. 10). Be sure the strands are flat and neat before tightening the knot. You are now quite familiar with the technique of braiding so that you can try a new braid. At this point you switch to the square braid. Hold the lanyard in the left hand, upside down, so that the strands fall apart and renumber then from 1 to 4 (Fig. 11).

Fold strand 1 over strand 2, leaving a small loop (Fig. 12). Hold it in position with the forefinger of the left hand. Hold each succeeding strand in position in the same way after each step. Fold strand 2 over strand 1 (Fig. 13).

Fold strand 3 over strand 2 (Fig. 14). Fold strand 4 over strand 3 and through the loop formed at the beginning (Fig. 15). Leave the stitch slightly loose (Fig. 16). Form the loop of the lanyard by folding the braid back and through the center of the square braid just formed (Fig. 17). Tighten the braid slightly.

Slide the square braid along the lanyard every few stitches to be certain that it is not too tight. Always keep it uniform and neat. Continue the square braid, using the lanyard as a core, until 4 inches of the strand are left. Renumber the strands after each stitch.

At this point you switch to the Terminal Turk's Head. In order to form a Terminal Turk's Head, leave the last stitch of the square braid slightly loose. Renumber the strands from 1 to 4 as shown in Fig. 17.

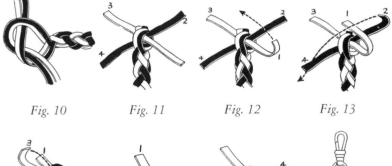

Fig. 10   Fig. 11   Fig. 12   Fig. 13

Fig. 14   Fig. 15   Fig. 16   Fig. 17

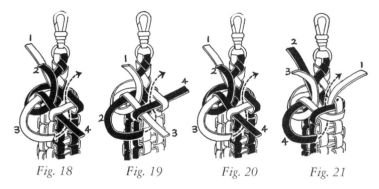

| Fig. 18 | Fig. 19 | Fig. 20 | Fig. 21 |

Hold the braid in the left hand. Bring strand 1 under strand 2 and up through the center. Leave this strand slightly loose (Fig. 18). All of the strands of the Terminal Turk's Head are to be tightened when the head is complete. Bring strand 2 under strand 3 and up through the center (Fig. 19).

Bring strand 3 under strand 4 and up through the center (Fig. 20). Bring strand 4 under strand 1 and 2 and up through the center (Fig. 21). Tighten the strands one at a time, starting with strand 1. A file, nailfile, nail or some other blunt pointed tool is a useful aid in tightening the strands. Tighten sufficiently to form a neat Terminal Turk's Head but loose enough to slide over the lanyard easily.

Be certain that none of the strands are twisted, then clip off the ends of the strands leaving a tassel of about 1 inch (Fig. 22). This completes the lanyard. An alternative to the Turk's Head Knot is made by stopping your weaving, as in Fig. 16, and tucking each strand into its own preceding stitch.

Fig. 22

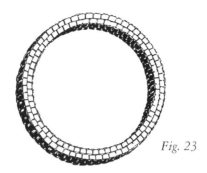

Fig. 23

✧ HOW TO MAKE A BRACELET ✧

In making a bracelet (Fig. 23) you can use the same type of gimp as used in making a lanyard. You can select the colors you like and make it any size you want. Like the lanyard you will require very little space to work in and you can accomplish a finished article the first time you set to work. Begin by using two strands of braid in the color desired, using about three yards of each color. Use the square braid, and pay careful attention to the illustrations.

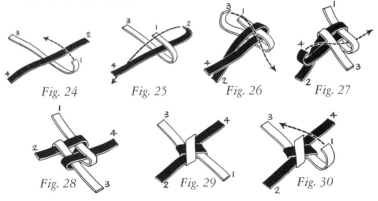

Fig. 24 *Fig. 25* *Fig. 26* *Fig. 27*

Fig. 28 *Fig. 29* *Fig. 30*

Fold strand 1 over strand 2, leaving a small loop (Fig. 24). Hold in position with the forefinger of the left hand. Hold each succeeding strand in position in the same way after each step. Fold strand 2 over strand 1 (Fig. 25). Fold strand 3 over strand 2 (Fig. 26). Fold strand 4 over strand 3 and through the loop formed at the beginning (Fig. 27). Keep the first stitch slightly loose. This completes the first stitch (Fig. 28).

It is now necessary to turn the braid upside down (Fig. 29). Then continue as before (Fig. 30). By doing this, a perfect square will appear at the end of the braid when both ends are ready to be joined (Fig. 31). Continue the square braid until the bracelet is the desired length. This can be determined by placing the bracelet on the wrist and bringing the two ends together. The bracelet is completed by interweaving the loose ends back into the beginning of the bracelet. The first stitch was left slightly loose so that the end strands can be interwoven into the beginning very easily.

Number the end strands 1 to 4 (Fig. 31). Then use a fid or some other blunt pointed tool to loosen one part of the first stitch. This will enable you to thread strand 1 into it as indicated by the dotted arrow in Fig. 32.

Then loosen another part of the first stitch and thread strand 2 into it as indicated by the dotted arrow in Fig. 33. Thread strand 3 into the first stitch following the dotted arrow in Fig. 34.

Thread strand 4 into the first stitch following the dotted arrow in Fig. 35. Tighten the strands in order, from 1 to 4, making sure each one is flat and neat. Then cut off the loose ends. The ending described above should be made so neat and blend so with the beginning with the braid, as to escape detection. This completes the bracelet (Fig. 36).

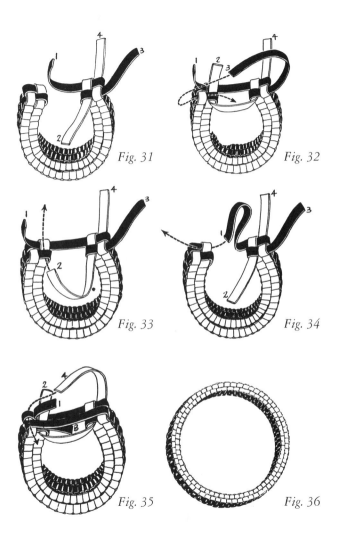

Fig. 31

Fig. 32

Fig. 33

Fig. 34

Fig. 35

Fig. 36

❖ KNOTTING ❖

Knotting has been one of the most popular pastimes of men in the Navy for generations, and many of our soldiers have taken to it as a hobby. This handicraft can be extremely interesting and a number of items can be made which can be used for gifts or for personal use.

Fig. 37

❖ HOW TO MAKE A SQUARE KNOT BELT ❖

To make this belt (Fig. 37) you will need a small buckle and 4 lengths of cord. The length of each piece of cord should be 7 times the length of the belt you wish to make. Hold the buckle with the tongue down and outside. Double one of the lengths of cord in the middle. Loop the end over the center bar of the buckle. Pass the ends of the cord through the loop and draw them tightly up as illustrated in Fig. 38. Do this with the other

Fig. 38

Fig. 39

three lengths of cord so that, when you have finished, your work looks like the illustration (Fig. 39).

Before you can begin to tie knots in the strands of cord you must have a way of holding them tight. The best way is shown in the illustration (Fig. 47). You can drive a nail into your workbench and put the buckle on it. To hold the strands tight you will wrap them around a nail on a board which you can hold between your knees. Now you are ready to make the knots.

Note, however, that each square knot has two parts. Each requires a separate step. To make a knot you must always use 4 strands of cord. First, use the four on the left of the tongue of the buckle and number them mentally as shown (Fig. 40). Here is the first half of making a knot. Take the two center strands (2 and 3) and wrap their ends around the nail in the board between your knees (as described). These strands must be kept tight at all times. Now take strand one in your left hand

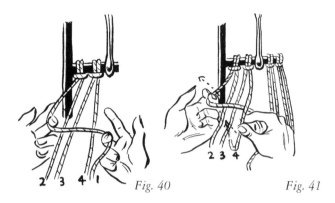

Fig. 40

Fig. 41

as shown in the illustration. With your right hand draw it over strands 2 and 3 and under stand 4. Take strand 4 between your right thumb and forefinger, as shown in the illustration (Fig. 41) and pass its end under strands 2 and 3 and into the loop of strand 1 (Fig. 41). Pull strands 1 and 4 tightly up on strands 2 and 3 as illustrated in Fig. 42. This completes the first half of one square knot.

To finish the knot, you will vary the procedure you followed in the first half. Take strand 4 and pass it under strands 2 and 3 and over strand 1 as shown in the illustration Fig. 43. Take

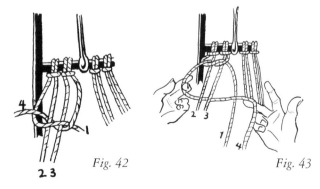

Fig. 42

Fig. 43

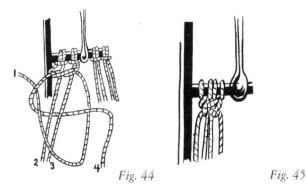

Fig. 44   *Fig. 45*

strand 1 and pass it over strands 2 and 3 and into the loop of strand 4. When you have finished this your work will look like the illustration Fig. 44. Then pull the strands tightly and the second half of your square knot is completed as illustrated in Fig. 45. To complete your first row of knots you will use the four strands to the right of the buckle tongue and follow the same procedure as in completing your first square knot.

After you have finished your first row of knots, you will want to vary your system so that all 8 strands of the belt are knotted together. This is done by continuing with the same

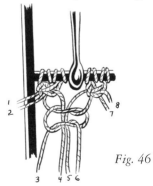

Fig. 46

type of square knots, working now with strands 3, 4, 5, and 6 (the four middle strands). Take strand 3 in your left hand, and with your right hand draw it over strands 4 and 5 and under strand 6. Take strand 6 between your right thumb and forefinger, and pull its ends under strands 4 and 5 and into the loop of strand 3 following the procedure as illustrated in Figs. 40 and 41. Pull strands 3 and 6 tightly up on strand 4 and 5. This completes the first half of one center square knot (Row 2).

Fig. 47

To finish the knot, you will vary the procedure you followed in the first half. Take strand 6, and pull it under 4 and 5 and over strand 3. Take strand 3 and pull it over strands 4 and 5 and into the loop of strand 6. At the completion of this step your work should look like Fig. 44. The 3rd row across and every other row of knots thereafter is tied with the same strands as the 1st row, namely strands 1, 2, 3, 4 for the 1st knot—5, 6, 7, 8 for the 2nd knot. The 4th row across and every other row of the knots thereafter is tied with the same strands as the 2nd row, namely 3, 4, 5, 6. This procedure is repeated until the desired length of the belt is obtained.

To finish, take strand 8 and bend it toward the center. Take strand 7 and pass it first over and then under strand 8 leaving a loop. Then pull the end of strand 8 down through the loop. In this way you have made a half-hitch. Repeat this procedure to make a double half-hitch. Make double half-hitches around strand 8 with strands 6 and 5. Take strand 1 and bend it toward the center. Make double half-hitches on it with strands 2, 3, and 5, and finally with strand 8 that you used for the first 3 half-hitches. When this is done, soak the half-hitches in water. This swells the fibers and causes the hitches to "set." Then cut off the loose ends of the strands close to the outer row of half-hitches. Your belt is now completed. No holes need be made for the tongue of the buckle as it can be slipped into one of the spaces already in the fabric of the belt.

FLY TYING

Fly tying is one of the most interesting and useful of all the handicrafts. It can be fun to do and it serves a practical purpose. This book will teach you in a practical way the methods whereby you can make a number of types of flies. The basic principle of fly tying is the decoration of a fish hook so that it will attract fish. There are two types of flies which can be used under different circumstances: wet and dry. The dry fly sets on top of the water while the wet fly usually rests under the surface. Flies can be designed to simulate actual insects or improvised to be completely artificial. To begin you must first know the different parts of the hook that you will use, Fig. 1. The hook is the primary basis of the fly.

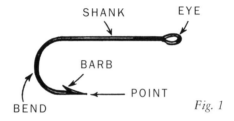

Fig. 1

The next thing to study are the different parts of the fly, Fig. 3.

You will need a few tools. Some of these can be made, but they can all be bought at a small cost. The first item you will need is a vise, Fig. 2. This is a cam lever type so that it can be made adjustable to various angles and hook sizes. The next item you will need is called Hackle Pliers, Fig. 2. You will also need a pair of scissors with very sharp points. The materials used for fly tying are varied and they cover a wide range. You will need a piece of wax, a spool of tying silk, a bottle of lacquer, and some silk floss. To make the body of the fly you will also require some wool yarn and chenille, a few sizes of tinsel for ribbing, an assortment of neck and saddle hackles, and some bucktails in three or four colors. There are a number of other materials that can be added later when you have mastered the fundamentals of fly tying.

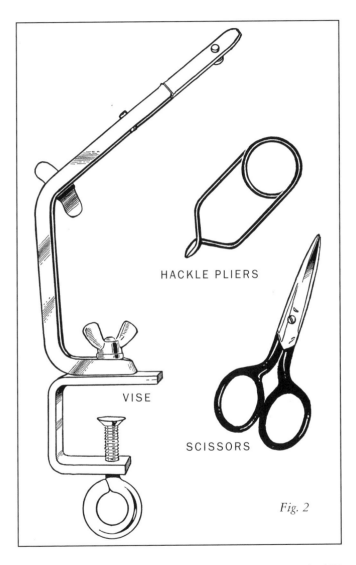

HACKLE PLIERS

VISE

SCISSORS

Fig. 2

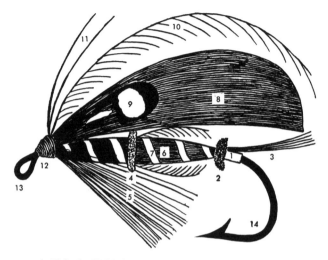

1: TAG, 2: BUTT, 3: TAIL, 4: JOINT, 5: HACKLE, 6: BODY,
7: RIBBING, 8: WING, 9: CHEEK, 10: TOPPING,
11: HORNS, 12: HEAD, 13: EYE, 14: HOOK

Fig. 3

✤ BUCKTAIL STREAMERS ✤

Now you can begin by placing a hook in the vise and start waxed tying silk, Fig. 4, ⅛ of an inch from the eye of the hook.

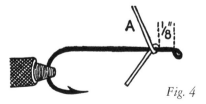

Fig. 4

Take five or six turns and cut off end, Fig. 5.

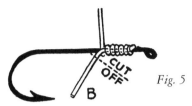

Fig. 5

Next wind tying silk closely and evenly down the shank of the hook, Fig. 6. Be sure you understand each step as you go along and work slowly at the beginning.

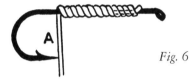

Fig. 6

The next step is important and a little more difficult; putting on the wings. Hold the tail material between your thumb and finger of the left hand. Slide the fingers down and over the hook so that the tail material rests on top of the hook, with the hook held firmly between your thumb and finger, Fig. 7.

Fig. 7

Next, loosen your grip a little to allow enough tying silk to pass between the thumb and tail material and down between the finger and material on the other side. Tighten your grip with thumb and finger and pull loop down tight, and repeat once more, Fig. 8.

Fig. 8

Now tie the tail in place with two turns of the tying silk (A) and tie in ribbing (D), Fig. 9.

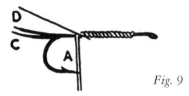

Fig. 9

Now take six or eight close tight turns with the tying silk towards the eye of the hook, and with two more turns tie in body material (E), Fig. 10. If you are using body tinsel, be sure to cut the end to a taper before tying in as (E) Fig. 10. This tends to make a smoother body and prevents a bunch where the material is tied in.

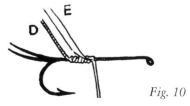

Fig. 10

Next wind tying silk (A) back to the starting point, take a half hitch and let it hang. Now wind body material (E) clockwise tightly and evenly back towards the barb, to the extreme rear end of the body; pull tight and wind forward to within ⅛ of an inch of the eye and wind back and forth to form smooth tapered body, Fig. 11. If using silk floss, untwist the floss and use only one-half or one-third strands; do not let it twist, wind tightly, and it will make a nice smooth body. Take two turns and a half hitch with the tying silk and cut off end of the material (F) Fig. 11. Take one tight turn with ribbing (D) over butt of tail close to rear of body, and also one turn under tail if tail is to be cocked.

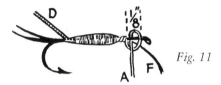

Fig. 11

Wind ribbing spirally around the body and tie off with two turns and a half hitch of tying silk, Fig. 12.

Fig. 12

Take about two dozen hairs of colored bucktail; cut off butt ends to the length wanted for the finished fly, not more than one half again as long as the hook, place these on top of the hook, Fig. 13, with butt ends about 1⁄16 of an inch in back of the eye.

Fig. 13

Pull down two or three loops, Fig 14. Now take about 1 to 5 hairs of other colored bucktail, and place them on top of the first colored bucktail the same as Fig. 13. Repeat the same operation as in Fig. 14. Before finishing the head put on a drop of head lacquer on the butt of the hairs to cement them in place.

Fig. 14

Finish up by making a smooth tapered head with the tying silk. Take three or four half hitches, paint the head with two or three coats of lacquer, and your fly is ready to use.

Fig. 15

✣ DRY FLIES ✣

This is one of the best all purpose flies. Begin by winding the tying silk ⅛ of an inch from the eye of the hook. Be sure your silk is waxed. Take two or three turns towards the bend of the hook and cut off the end, Fig. 16.

Fig. 16

Next cut a section about ¼ of an inch from a right and left wing feather, Fig. 17. If you can, use duck wings as these are best for dry flies.

Do not cut off the butt ends, but straddle the hook, Fig. 18.

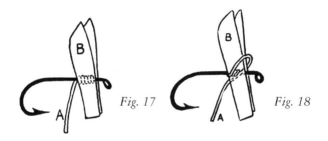

Fig. 17

Fig. 18

Tip the wings forward perpendicular to the shank and pull down the loop, Fig. 19.

Take one more turn with the silk and before loosening the grip with the left hand take two turns around the hook close behind the wings, Fig. 20.

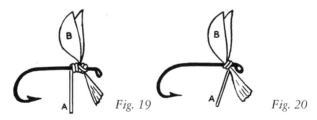

Fig. 19

Fig. 20

Now pull the butt ends back tightly as in Fig. 21, take two tight turns around them and cut off at dotted line.

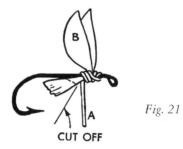

Fig. 21

Cross between wings to spread them, and wind tying silk down shank of the hook, Fig. 22.

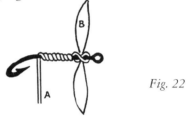

Fig. 22

From now on the body is made as previously explained, so for the sake of variation we will tie a band in the center the same as a Royal Coachman. Tie in tail, Fig. 23.

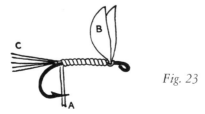

Fig. 23

Tie in two or three strands of peacock herl, Fig. 24, and wind four or five turns towards the eye of the hook.

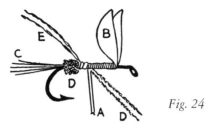

Fig. 24

Take three or four strands of silk floss, Fig. 25, and take a few more turns over the loose ends towards the eye of the hook. Wind silk floss over the herl about half way up the hook.

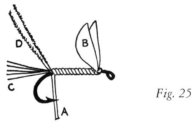

Fig. 25

Take a turn or two around silk floss and cut off end, Fig. 26. Carry up to the front of the wings.

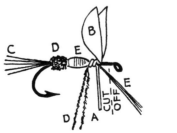

Fig. 26

Finish body with herl wound tight against the back of the wings. (This helps to push the wings forward and to hold them in place.) Tie off herl, Fig. 27.

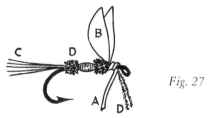

Fig. 27

The next step of putting on the hackle is done as shown in Fig. 21. The hackle is much more important than on the wet fly. The floating qualities of the dry fly depend almost entirely upon stiff neck hackle of the right size. Often two hackles are used, laid together, with both butts tied in at the same time. One hackle of the proper size and stiffness is usually enough, so we will use one tied as in Fig. 18. and explained in Fig. 21. Clip the hackle pliers to the tip of hackle and wind about two turns edgewise in front of the wings, then, wind two turns close in back of the wings. Take two or three more turns in front of the wings, keeping the hackle edgewise, with the shiny side towards the eye of the hook. Wind the hackle close so as not to fill up the eye of the hook, and so as to leave room for the head. Tie in the tip with a couple of turns, Fig. 28.

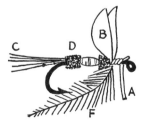

Fig. 28

The hackle should now be standing straight out from the hook, with most of it in front of the wings. Now shape a tapered head. Head should be about ¹⁄₁₆ inch long on a size 12 hook, Fig. 29.

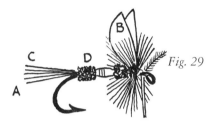

Fig. 29

Finish with two or three half hitches and a drop of head lacquer, Fig. 30.

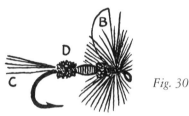

Fig. 30

Various types of feathers are used for wings of dry flies. The best are breast feathers from mallard, teal, partridge, grouse, black duck, or wood duck. Hackle tips, starling, duck, turkey, goose pheasant, wing feathers, etc.

Two whole feathers of the proper size with the natural curve are used for fan wings. The tips of two feathers, or a section may be cut from two matched feathers. All of these wings are tied on in the same manner as previously explained.

❖ FLOATING BUGS ❖

One of the greatest attractions for fish are Floating Bugs. These can be made of a variety of materials. Let us begin by making a simple one. If you follow the instructions carefully and look at the illustrations you will be rewarded in your first effort by an effective Floating Bug. As in other procedures, remember to wax your silk thoroughly. Take a few turns around the shank of the hook and tie in a small bunch of hairs for the tail. See Fig. 31.

Fig. 31

Now clip a small bunch of hairs about the size of a match, close to the hide. If there is some fuzz mixed with the hair at the base close to the skin pick out the fuzz and place the butts of the hairs under the hook, Fig. 32.

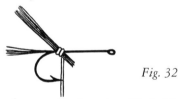

Fig. 32

Now take a couple of turns with the tying silk, hold the tips of the hair with the thumb and finger of the left hand, and pull the tying silk tight. Notice that the hairs spin around the hook and the butt ends stand out at right angles to the hook, Fig. 33.

Fig. 33

Now cut off the tip ends of the hairs and then press them back tightly. Apply a drop of lacquer to the base of the hairs and the hook, and repeat the same process of tying on a small bunch of hair, each time pressing it back slightly. Remember that the hair must be close together to make a smooth, even body. Your body should now be built up so that it looks like Fig. 34.

Fig. 34

At this stage remove it from your vise and with your scissors trim it so that it looks like Fig. 35 and 36. Now you should have about 3/16-inch of the hook's shank left just behind the eye.

Fig. 35

Fig. 36

This is where you will tie on your wings. Cover this bare hook with well waxed tying silk and lay a bunch of hair on top of the hook for wings, Fig. 37.

Fig. 37

Fig. 38

Criss cross the silk around the wings and the hook until they are firmly tied. Put on several coats of lacquer over the juncture of the wings and the hook so that they will remain secure. After you have lacquered the wings, let them dry. Then press them flat and trim them as shown in Fig. 38.

You now have a completed bug. You can create your own designs using any color you want to suit your own fancy.

✥ HOW TO WIND A ROD ✥

Here is a chance to own a real fishing rod. All you need is a long piece of bamboo, cut to the length you like. If bamboo is not available where you are, any type of wood which has a certain flexibility will serve the purpose. The principles of winding to make a high class rod are described simply. Follow each step carefully and take notice of the illustrations.

Although it is somewhat exacting work, anyone with a little patience can learn to wind a rod. Put a spool on a nail and drive the nail into a block of wood. Bend the nail slightly to secure desired tension and place the spool or spools at your right. Mark the places for guides and in-between winding on flat or top side of rod.

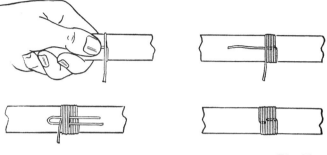

Fig. 39

Hold the rod in the left hand with one end supported between the elbow and body. The right hand is to assist the left in holding and turning it and to guide the silk on the rod.

About three inches from the end of the silk, loop it around the rod to the left with the loose end extended toward you. The portion of the silk extending to the spool should overlap the loose end. Place the tip of a finger where they cross and turn the stick until you see it is going to hold.

During the winding the silk must be kept tight.

After about three complete turns of the rod, take a razor blade or a sharp knife and trim the loose end close to the last turn of the silk. Take this small piece and fold it back against itself making a loop. Place this between the rod and the thread extending to the spool with the loop end toward you. Continue to wind over this loop for at least three turns, then place thumb on the silk to keep it from unwinding and cut the thread about two inches from the rod. Insert the loose end through the loop and pull it back under the winding. Pull the end carefully to be sure the winding is tight, then cut off as close to the silk as possible, in order not to injure the winding.

CARTOONING

More people read the newspaper comics than any other feature and many popular magazines use cartoons to liven up their pages. Except for a few syndicates, feature services are on the lookout for cartoons, and pay good money for them.

Practice and patience can make you a cartoonist. Maybe you remember when you learned to write. It took a little while before people could read your writing. Try the same thing now with cartoons, just using a pencil, some paper, and the simple lessons of this booklet. If necessary, copy some of the drawings at first to *feel* how it's done. As you go along notice how the professional gets certain effects. No one ever became a cartoonist overnight so don't become discouraged if your own efforts don't look professional immediately. *Practice* in pencil first and later swing into pen and ink work. Study established strips and cartoons for new techniques and popular trends, then develop a style of your own.

✤ THE TOOLS ✤

Cartoons require little equipment. Some of the best work has been done with a piece of scrap paper and a penny's worth of black ink. From your Special Services officer get some drawing pens, (Gillott's 170, 290, and 404) and an oval point writing pen, and some very soft, soft and medium pencils, a pad of tracing paper 9 × 12, drawing paper 9 × 12 (Bristol board for pen and ink work), soft and hard erasers, a bottle of India ink, some correction fluid for touching up errors, and a pen holder. Later on add a ruler, T-square and drawing board.

These pages have been divided into the subjects every cartoonist should master. Study each and practice making drawings of the features, body and action. Continue practicing your composition and perspective long after you've mastered pen and ink techniques, since those are the most technical problems in cartooning as well as any other art.

Take your time! Don't rush. You want to get as much fun out of this as you can while you're learning.

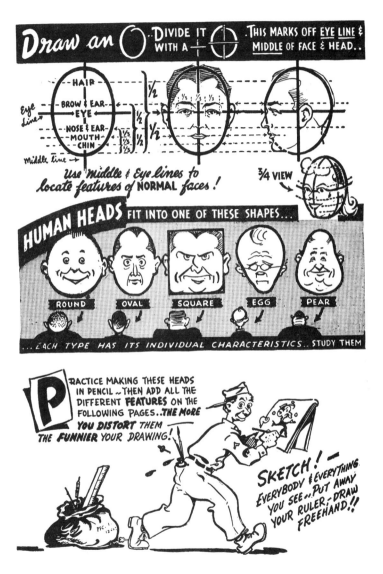

Draw an ○ . DIVIDE IT WITH A + ⊕ . THIS MARKS OFF <u>EYE LINE</u> & <u>MIDDLE</u> OF FACE & HEAD..

HAIR
BROW & EAR
EYE
NOSE & EAR
MOUTH
CHIN

Eye Line →

Middle line →

½ ½ ½ ½

⅓ ⅓ ⅓

⅓ ⅓ ⅓

Use middle & Eye lines to locate features of NORMAL faces!

¾ VIEW

HUMAN HEADS FIT INTO ONE OF THESE SHAPES...

ROUND   OVAL   SQUARE   EGG   PEAR

...EACH TYPE HAS ITS INDIVIDUAL CHARACTERISTICS.. STUDY THEM

PRACTICE MAKING THESE HEADS IN PENCIL ~ THEN ADD ALL THE DIFFERENT **FEATURES** ON THE FOLLOWING PAGES.. *THE MORE* *YOU DISTORT* THEM THE *FUNNIER* YOUR DRAWING!

SKETCH ! —
EVERYBODY & EVERYTHING
YOU SEE.. PUT AWAY
YOUR RULER - DRAW
FREEHAND!!

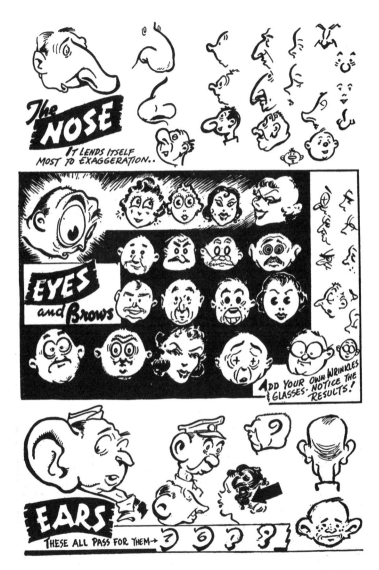

The NOSE

IT LENDS ITSELF MOST TO EXAGGERATION..

EYES and Brows

ADD YOUR OWN WRINKLES & GLASSES. NOTICE THE RESULTS!

EARS

THESE ALL PASS FOR THEM →

CARTOONING *the* FEMALE

1.

2.

Simple Way to make Girls Face

They're NOT ALL Pin Ups!

ROUGH IN A SKELETON 8 HEADS TALL...

1 2 3 4 5 6 7 8

1 2 3 4 5 6 7 8 9

Accentuate GRACE with long CLEAN LINES, MAKE THIGHS & LEGS LONGER.

...THEN ROUND OUT THE FIGURE

CLOTHES MAKE THE WOMAN

NOTE HOW A FEW LINES INDICATE CLOTHING..

A High Skirt gives Youthful appearance

Folds follow Body Contours

Keep up with the Fashion News for New STYLES.

Comic **ANIMALS**

USE SKELETON FIGURES TO SKETCH IN YOUR ACTION ....

ROUGH IN THE FRAMEWORK...

BODIES OF THE **DOG** FAMILY (WOLF, FOX, ETC) FIT INTO **SQUARES**

..THEN MODEL IN THE FINISHED FIGURE

CATS (LIONS, TIGERS, ETC.) FIT INTO **OBLONGS**

...**PUT HUMAN EXPRESSIONS ON YOUR ANIMALS TO MAKE THEM LOOK FUNNY!**

INK

Practice ALL THESE PEN AND BRUSH STROKES.

..THEN INK IN
YOUR PENCIL
SKETCHES·

TECHNIQUES

ALL THESE LINES
½ ORIGINAL SIZE

DRAWN WITH ORDINARY BALL POINTED PEN

DRAWN WITH GILLOTT'S
PENS #170, 290, 404.. &
HUNT PENS #22, 99, 56.
(USE *BRISTOL BOARD* FOR INKING)

DRAWN WITH #4 SABLE BRUSH.

LIGHT & SHADOW

THROW LIGHT BEAMS AROUND OBJECTS
& SKETCH THE SHADOWS...

HIGH
LIGHT--
SHORT
SHADOW---

LOW LIGHT
LONG
SHADOW→

GOOD EXAMPLE
LIGHT & SHADOW
USING PEN STROKES

EFFECTIVE USE OF LIGHT
& SHADOW TO MOLD FIGURES
AND CHARACTER..
(ADVENTURE STRIP STYLE)

SHADING

EXPERIMENT WITH DIFFERENT PATTERNS.. USE SHADING TO EMPHASIZE YOUR PEOPLE OR OBJECTS.

SIMPLE SOLIDS PREFERRED BY THE MAGAZINES

THE SAME GUY IN SLAPSTICK

A STYLE STILL LIKED BY SOME CARTOONISTS

DRAPERY AND WRINKLES..

ADVENTURE STRIP STYLE (BRUSH)

SIMPLE CARTOON STYLE (PEN)

NOTICE HOW FOLDS IN THE CENTER(Y) FORM BETWEEN HIGH POINTS WHERE THERE ARE PULL & TENSION (X)

SHOWING WRINKLES ON BLACK →

Some Cartoonists never use wrinkles – but their lines show lots of **ACTION!**

Simple COMPOSITION

COMPOSE YOUR CARTOON TO PLACE YOUR MAIN FIGURES IN THE SPOTLIGHT (PRACTICE THIS)

THIS PART OF YOUR DRAWING ATTRACTS THE EYE FIRST ...

Bad -- FIGURES & OBJECTS DIVIDE PICTURE INTO UNINTERESTING QUARTERS.

Bad ... WALLS, DOOR AND HORIZON CHOP OFF THE HEADS ... WHILE BORDERS SLICE THE BODIES TOO MUCH

BETTER - BUT NOT GOOD .. CLOUDS, HORIZON & RIVER BANK FORM TOO MANY HORIZONTALS........

GOOD .. MAIN FIGURES IN SPOTLIGHT .. OTHER LINES POINT TO THEM -

GOOD .. DOG EMPHASIZED BY SIZE AND FULL FACED ACTION CREATES SPOTLIGHT.

WATER

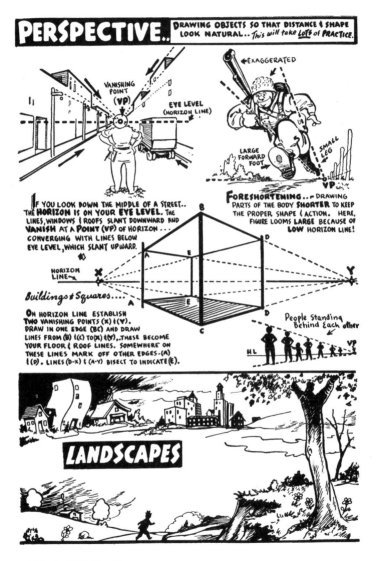

PERSPECTIVE..

DRAWING OBJECTS SO THAT DISTANCE & SHAPE LOOK NATURAL.. This will take Lots of PRACTICE.

VANISHING POINT (VP)

EYE LEVEL (HORIZON LINE)

←EXAGGERATED

LARGE FORWARD FOOT

SMALL LEG

VP

IF YOU LOOK DOWN THE MIDDLE OF A STREET.. THE HORIZON IS ON YOUR EYE LEVEL. THE LINES, WINDOWS & ROOFS SLANT DOWNWARD AND **VANISH** AT A POINT (VP) OF HORIZON ... CONVERGING WITH LINES BELOW EYE LEVEL, WHICH SLANT UPWARD.

FORESHORTENING.. ┌ DRAWING PARTS OF THE BODY **SHORTER** TO KEEP THE PROPER SHAPE & ACTION. HERE, FIGURE LOOMS **LARGE** BECAUSE OF **LOW** HORIZON LINE!

HORIZON LINE→

B

D

E

A

Buildings & Squares....

ON HORIZON LINE ESTABLISH TWO VANISHING POINTS (X) & (Y). DRAW IN ONE EDGE (BC) AND DRAW LINES FROM (B) & (C) TO (X) & (Y)..THESE BECOME YOUR FLOOR & ROOF LINES. SOMEWHERE ON THESE LINES MARK OFF OTHER EDGES–(A) & (D). LINES (D–X) & (A–Y) BISECT TO INDICATE (E).

A

E

D

C

Y

People Standing Behind Each other

H L

VP

LANDSCAPES

EXAGGERATE KID FOREHEADS. EYE LINE RISES TO CENTER AS CHILD GROWS OLDER.

KIDS.. HEIGHT RANGES FROM 4 TO 7 HEADS

TEEN AGE CARTOONS ARE GROWING IN POPULARITY.

THINK BACK TO YOUR OWN CHILDHOOD FOR GOOD KID MATERIAL ...

LETTERING

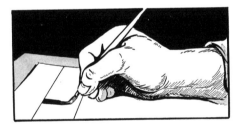

For your own amusement you may enjoy making personal monograms or lettering your friend's equipment. In the commercial field you will find lettering the backbone of advertising, whether it be the showcard for the corner drug store, the department store display, the billboards, or the swell looking ad in the slick magazine. Even the comic strip artists hire good lettering men to letter the "balloons" of their cartoons.

✧ TAKE YOUR TIME ✧

You can learn to letter as you learned to write… all it takes is *patience*, practice, and more *practice*. The hints given here are short-cuts of the profession. Follow them step by step—keeping at it until you can do it all easily and without referring to the booklet.

✧ BASIC TOOLS ✧

Ask your Special Services Officer for the following materials which should be a part of your equipment, together with a pad of tracing paper, assorted showcards, and smooth Bristol board.
- a drawing board
- assorted pencils, (3H, 2H, H, B, 2B, and 3B)
- Chisel point pencils, No. 2B, 3B, and 6B
- Gillotte pens No. 170 and No. 303
- assorted Speedball pens
- 3 penholders
- Square tip brushes No. 4 through 10
- Pointed tip brushes No. 2 and No. 3
- assorted inks and poster colors
- black waterproof ink
- art gum and kneaded erasers
- ink eraser and some tacks
- a ruler
- a T-Square and triangle

❖ **PRACTICE DRILLS** ❖

Rule off four parallel lines ¼-inch apart and do these preliminary exercises with a round Speedball pen.

Then perform these drills over and over again.

It may seam boring at first, but it's going to pay off later. Notice your wrist movement? The way you hold your pen? How the point of the lettering pen rests flat on the paper? Try it again now and notice the improvement already.

Now try the same exercises with a chisel point pencil, increasing you guide line spaces to ½-inch apart.

Practice now with different size brushes for large single strokes. Here you will notice a combined *arm* and *wrist* motion. Your brush will be held like a pen bearing down until half its length touches the paper.

When the brush is drawn toward you, your finger pressure relaxes and as it reaches the bottom guide line the brush will assume an almost vertical position, leaving a square cut edge on the drawn line.

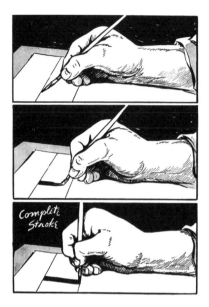

✤ JOIN THE BASIC STROKES ✤

Combine the strokes you learned on pages 161-163 and combine them to form letters. Do them freehand. Don't rush. Speed will come with practice. Note the direction of each stroke and order in which each is made to form a letter. Memorize them as you go along. First try the capital letters, then the small letters, after which combine them all to form words.

No matter how professional you may become—you will find that some of your brush or Speedball pen strokes will leave ragged edges. For the purpose of "sharpening up" the letters, use your drawing pens (No. 170 and No. 303).

✤ SIMPLICITY AND LEGIBILITY ✤

Most of our modern lettering stems from Roman and Gothic alphabets most common to our Western civilization. The simpler they are made the better they can be read. Hand lettering has more appeal to the eye because it is more flexible than mechanical type. Each letter must be shaped and spaced to become a part of an attractive design, otherwise your sign is worthless.

The alphabets on the facing page are among the three most popular types used by advertisers today. Notice their simplicity and legibility.

To the right, you will see three types of lettering. The first is a classic Roman alphabet, suitable for signage of all kinds. The second is a condensed Gothic type, which is a bit more modern style favored by some artists. The third type is a script style appropriate for cartoons.

Page 168 illustrates several simple Gothic alphabets. Notice the effect of serifs on the lower three lines.

Page 169 illustrates an Old English and a Roman script, with a suggestion for guide lines for fine lettering.

Fig. 1

ABCDEFGHIJKLMNOPQRSTUV
WXYZ   1234567890
abcdefghijklmnopqrstuvwxyz

ABCDEFGHIJKLMNOPQRSTUV
WXYZ   1234567890
abcdefghijklmnopqrstuvwxyz

ABCDEFGHIJKLMNOPQRSTUV
WXYZ   1234567890
abcdefghijklmnopqrstuvwxyz

A B C D E F G H I J K L M N O P
Q R S T U V W X Y Z a b c d e f g
h i j k l m n o p q r s t u v w x y z

ABCDEFGHIJKLMNOPQRSTUV
WXYZ   1234567890
abcdefghijklmnopqrstuvwxyz

ABCDEFGHIJ
KLMNOPQRS
TUVWXYZ
abcdefghijklmn
opqrstuvwxyz

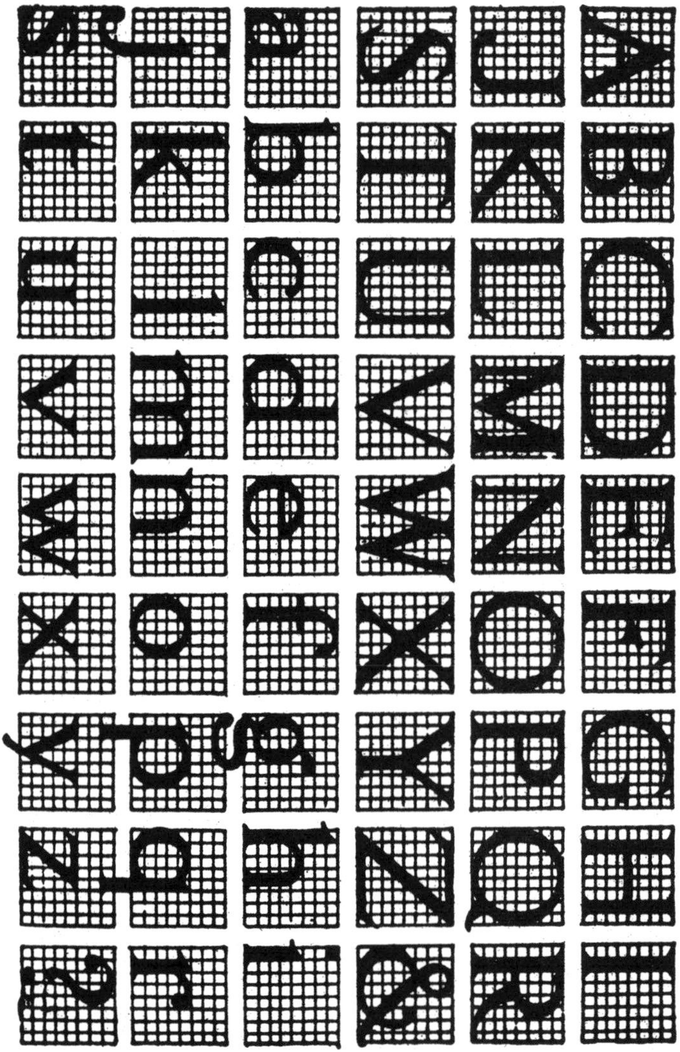

Fig. 2

✤ SPACING AND PROPORTIONS ✤

Spacing and proportions are important factors in making your sign or poster. The area of white space, not the distance between letters, must be the same for properly spaced words. Fig. 2 illustrates the different sizes of letters in their exact proportions. Because of the differences in sizes you cannot resort to mechanical spacing.

This area of space must also take into consideration the white space within open letters. This cannot be done with a ruler. Train your eye to judge proper "color" formed by little blocks of letters forming words. The typewriter is a good example of mechanical spacing. Notice the word "SLIMMER" and how some parts of the word seem to fall away. This is improved by letter spacing and adding a serif (tail).

Before drawing your lettering on the Bristol board or card-

SLIMMER

SLIMMER

board, plan your "ROUGH" on a sheet of tracing paper marked off in proportion to your sign. Indicate your guide lines and then pencil in your lettering.

(SPACES IN THESE LETTERS ARE TOO LARGE)

BAD SPACING ←→

Squint your eyes. Does it look spotty? Darker in one area than another? Now is your chance to change and improve it. Erase wherever necessary.

Rearrange your lines, expand or condense or make the strokes thinner or thicker, or you may find it advisable to get more distance between each letter. Whatever you decide to do, this is the time to do it, but be sure the change is uniform for the entire word, line or paragraph. You may notice that the more condensed the letter, the taller it appears.

NOTICE HOW THE BLACKS (INDICATING SPACE BETWEEN LETTERS) SEEM EVEN, ALTHOUGH SOME LETTERS ARE ACTUALLY CLOSER TOGETHER (P–A, C–I).

When the "Rough" is finished, rub down the back of the tracing paper with a soft pencil and trace down the lettering on the Bristol board or cardboard with a hard pencil. Don't press too hard, you'll hurt the surface of your cardboard.

Go over the lines again on the cardboard with a medium soft pencil and proceed to ink in with pen or brush. If you use the outline method (top line of Fig. 3) fill in each word as you go along so you can judge the proper weight of the letters. (bottom line of Fig. 3.) Serifs (little tails) may be added to the letters to create a different alphabet to lend the right "color."

Fig. 3

These processes may seem drawn out at first but you will find that it will save you grief and time. It will make your work look professional.

✤ POSTERS ✤

Posters or large advertisements composed entirely of lettering or combined with an illustration, require good composition and layout. This is an art in itself and many lettering men specialize as layout men. Layouts can make or break the ad. Use the tracing paper method. Cut out the blocks of lettering as roughed in, and a sketch of the illustration. Rearrange them around the board. Squint your eyes at the overall design. If it satisfies you, transfer to the drawing paper or cardboard, and ink in your work.

Choice of lettering should be made carefully to suit the product you're selling. An appeal to women will be in dainty and distinct lettering. Men will be reached with a bold powerful alphabet. Your lettering will shout a warning or tease you gently with a whispering headline. It will set the reader's mood. See Fig. 4. *Study* lettering in magazine ads. Clip them and save them in a "research file" for future use.

Fig. 4

✦ HINTS AND TRICKS OF THE TRADE ✦

1. *Always wash your brushes* as soon as you've finished with them.

2. *If your Speedball pens become caked with ink,* just scrape off the tips with a knife or razor blade. Dipping them in ammonia will also remove the ink.

3. *Glossy showcards often do not take your ink very well.* If you come across such paper—simply wash the board lightly with plain GI soap suds and water.

4. *In transferring your material* from the tracing paper to the poster board, don't tack it down. Rub some GI soap on each corner of the tracing paper and it will adhere to the board without slipping.

5. *Color is important in your work.* Use it wisely so that it attracts attention to the message of your sign.

6. *On white—black paint shows up best,* then come brown, blue, green and red. Don't use yellow on white—it doesn't show up well. Good contrasting color combinations are black and yellow, yellow and blue, and yellow and red.

❖ INDEX ❖